المعلقات العشر

THE SEVEN GOLDEN ODES OF PAGAN ARABIA

Wilfrid Scawen Blunt

Qadeem Press

Qadeem Press

Qadeem Press Edition
Breathing Life into Forgotten Pages
www.qadeempress.com

CONTENTS.

	PAGE
INTRODUCTION	ix
IMR-EL-KÁIS	1
TÁRAFA	9
ZOHÉYR	17
LEBÍD .	24
ÁNTARA .	31
IBN KOLTHÜM	37
EL HÁRITH	44
NOTES .	51

DEDICATED

TO

FREDERICK YORK POWELL

IN TOKEN OF AN OLD FRIENDSHIP AND OF MUCH

ORIENTAL SYMPATHY

INTRODUCTION

THE ancient poetry of Arabia, immediately before the advent of Mohammed, is the most delightful wild flower of literature the Eastern world can show. Compared with it, all other Asiatic verse has a certain garden character, the bravery of the cultured rose and jessamine and lily. But this has the fugitive beauty of the lily of the field, nay, of something wilder still, the flower of no field at all but of the naked desert, which after the spring rain is clothed for an instant with diminutive strange blossoms peculiar to itself and which are seen no more. All that it can be likened to with any justice is the lyrical portion of the older Hebrew scriptures—parts of the Book of Job, the Psalms of David without their piety, the love-canticle of Solomon without its mystic meaning. In Europe the nearest analogy to it is perhaps to be found in the pre-Christian verse of Celtic Ireland, which by a strange accident was its close contemporary, and lost its wild natural impulse through the very same circumstance of the conversion of its pagan bards to an overmastering new theology.

Of its quite early history we know nothing except that it would seem to have been an indigenous product of the Arabian soil, not unconnected with the primaeval civilization of Yemen, and that it had acquired a new importance through the historical dispersion of the Yemenite clans in the second century of the Christian era and the founding of the two Arabian kingdoms of the north, Ghassán and Híra. At the time when the earliest poems of which we have any record were composed, that is to say, some three centuries later, the whole of the Peninsula was in the occupation of more or less kindred pastoral communities, following the same customs, speaking the same language, and bound by the same code of honour in peace and war. Each tribal section had its own *díra*, or pasturing district, beyond whose limits its flocks and herds did not wander, nor the tents of its women. The chief men, however, of whatever clan, were not thus to be confined, and, besides the raids of many hundred miles they made in wartime, travelled far afield in time of peace, and, wherever there was no blood feud, passed from tribe to tribe, enjoying hospitality, seeking adventures, and reciting, with what talent they had, their verses. As such singers and warriors became known and their fame spread abroad, there sprang up a competition among the tribe sheykhs to receive them, and especially the Arab kings of Híra and Ghassán liked to attract them to their Courts. It gave these princes an intellectual amusement to be thus surrounded, flattered their vanity and enlarged their influence. It was through the medium of the two rival Courts of the north that the poets of Arabia got indirectly their knowledge of the world outside. The Prince of Híra was tributary to the *Késra* (Chrosroes) of Persia, and the Prince of Ghassán was tributary in like manner to the *Kaísar* (Caesar) of Byzantine Rome. Faint echoes of the resplendent imperial names are to be heard in the Arabian poetry, but they are echoes only, coming from afar and received at second hand.

It is not difficult for any one who has travelled in modern Nejd to form to himself a picture of what these princely Courts then were. They cannot have differed much from those of the Ibn Saóuds and the Ibn Rashíds of to-day. The Prince, half Bedouin half townsman, was in his desert quality still *sheykh* of his own noble tribe enriched by his bounties. In the city where he had built himself a fortress, he was *hákim*, its lord and king. He took his tribute in the desert through the might of his camel and horse riders. He took his tax of the settled population of the desert edge through the *fedawín*, his Arab guard of foot-soldiers. The winter months of cold and the extreme heats of summer saw him delivering public justice daily in his castle; the spring and autumn saw him in his tents, or on horseback making foray on his enemies. The Arab strangers came and went, were entertained and departed as they would, some singing his praises for largesse received, others in dudgeon because neglected, all alike defiant of authority in act and word. They were hawks of too wild a plumage to be reclaimed by threats or cajoleries into permanent service. Thus at the present day one finds, even now in England-ridden Egypt, certain Bedouins from Central Arabia, waifs from the noble tribes of Mutéyr and Harb and Atéybeh, always clustered in semi-service round the Khedivial Court at Koubba. Here and there among them may be discovered a poet, here and there a *rebâb* player; all are horsemen. They come and serve for a while as *râkibîn* (riders) to mount and break the Khedivial colts or the Khedivial camels. They are ornamental apparitions in their gay dresses and equipments, are good horse-masters and honest in their service. But manual labour they will not condescend to do, nor will they be drilled as soldiers, nor sleep in houses, nor wear uniforms. At the least huff they are away. They go forth from the palace outspoken in the Prince's blame or praise, nor will money tempt them back nor the thought of fear or favour.

In their own land the *Poets of the Ignorance*, for such is the name given them by Islamic writers, were sometimes themselves princes or of princely family. They were at least free gentlemen of blood and lineage, undebased by toil and ignoring the "dignity of labour." They were warriors and knights errant, the heroes of their own romances, prompt with sword and spear, horsemen and camel-riders, tent-dwellers from their childhood and inured to physical hardships of all kinds. Outdoor doers of wild deeds, these valorous desert song-masters were no mere decadents, the "idle singers of an empty day," but men determined to live every hour of their gay lives, to enjoy every joy within their reach to their pleasure's uttermost. Here we find nothing of the Ossianic gloom of our own archaic bards, nothing of the superstitious doubts and conscience-stricken terrors of mediaeval Europe in fear of things beyond the grave, nothing of the theological limitations of the later Moslem verse. All with them is frankly, inspiritingly, stupendously hedonistic.

The primitive Arabs, just as are still their true Bedouin descendants, were rank materialists. They believed in neither heaven nor hell, nor in any life beyond the one they were enjoying. Of religion they understood nothing but a vague monotheism, tempered with just enough idolatry to make oath by, but not enough to modify their lives. They were the least superstitious of mankind, the least influenced by fetish fears and hobgoblin terrors. It was their habit to be abroad at night or to sit round their camp-fires under the stars in mirth and song, and then to sleep by day, a mode of living which gave but little room for idle ghost fancies born of indoor ways and the dread of darkness. There was none of that fear of loneliness, that awe of mountain solitudes that for thousands of years haunted the European mind, and made the snowfields of the Alps and the great pine forests of Germany the fearful home of fabulous powers and shapes to be avoided. It is the townsman in the East, the dweller in houses of stone and brick, that trembles at the thought of the Jinns, not he whose dwelling is the "house of hair." The Bedouin knows his deserts far too well to be afraid. He has been too often alone in his mountains night and day to dream that they are unnaturally inhabited. The noises he hears in the darkness he reads the next morning, as in a book, explained by the tracks left by the night prowler in the sand. There is no sound, no voice in all the desert that he does not recognize as one familiar from his childhood, and always to be accounted for by natural causes. Why then should he be afraid? The absence of the supernatural is the distinguishing feature, as contrasted with all other primitive poetries, of the poetry of the Arabian Ignorance.

In morals, the pre-Islamic Arabs, in spite of certain lapses, stood notably higher than any of their neighbours in Asia. It must be remembered, however, that their rule of conduct was based upon no religious sanction, but avowedly on personal and tribal honour, that is to say, on traditional opinion. The virtues they adored were courage, generosity, lavish hospitality, the protection of the weak and of all who came to them as suppliants, a readiness to succour a friend and revenge a wrong, a prompt self-sacrifice for the tribe's sake in peace or war. Their courage was of a different quality, perhaps, from that admired among ourselves. It was the valour of a nervous, excitable people who required encouragement from onlookers and from their own voices to do their best, defiance before the battle, immoderate boasting afterwards. It needed not seldom the taunts of their women to make them face their foes or stop their flight. It is still the custom in cases of warfare of a serious kind in Arabia for the tribe to take its womenfolk with it on a campaign, as obliging even the laggards to fight manfully, and they have a girl accompanying them mounted on a camel who sings and shouts to them during the combat. Thus worked upon, the tribesmen fear neither death nor wounds, and become heroic. So, too, with their generosity, there is always in it an element of vainglory which finds strengthening in the presence of friends. A great sheykh, even if he is secretly parsimonious, will give prodigally in public out of regard for his neighbours' eyes, for the fame of an open hand gains many adherents. The motive is perhaps not a high one, yet it is a wholesome thing in any society that to give should be counted of more glory than to keep, and with some among them the freehandedness is very real. The true mastering virtue, however, of Arabia is its hospitality. There, it would be a shame for the poorest and meanest to refuse a stranger, nor would any, though he were alone, turn such away from his tent-door. Conscience would step in and prevent so great a failure of honour. Another matter of *conscience* is the blood revenge. This in a noble Arabian mind becomes a passionate prompting, almost a physical necessity, which if it be not obeyed will deprive its subject of sleep, of appetite, of health, and leave him a miserable man. On the same footing, in a minor degree, stand the duties of succouring the weak and protecting suppliants who have thrown themselves beneath the protector's cloak, even should he be an enemy. In all these instances a well-born Arab will act on principles which it would be idle not to recognize as moral, yet which are neither held as binding by Moslems in general, nor are practised with fidelity anywhere else in western Asia but only in Arabia.

Towards women, the Arabs of the Ignorance were at the same time devoted and practical. The girls and matrons of the tribe were no slaves or chattels, as in primitive Europe, but essentially free-born women with their right of choice before marriage, and of leaving the domestic hearth, if dissatisfied, after marriage. They were made much of by the men, and enjoyed a better social position not only than the women in most other lands of the pagan East, but also than those of contemporary Christendom. Many of them were as courageous and as well educated, if the word can be used of a people who none of them could read or write, as their husbands or their lovers. The Arabs, therefore, had in their womenkind the material of a high romance, and they built on it the whole scheme of chivalry which we are accustomed to consider an exclusively Christian condition of things, but which in fact mediaeval Europe imitated and developed on lines of its own from the original Arab model, brought through

Africa into Spain. Knight-errantry, the riding forth on horseback in search of adventures, the rescue of captive maidens, the succour rendered everywhere to women in adversity, all these were essentially Arabian ideas, as was the very name of *chivalry*, the connection of honourable conduct with the horse-rider, the man of noble blood, the cavalier. Genealogy, the pride of lineage, the belief in the quality of blood ancestrally inherited as something superior either to riches or to any other accidental advantage, and conferring on its owner moral characteristics impossible of acquisition by the vulgar, were no less essentially Arabian and, if found at all elsewhere than among the Arabs, were nowhere so intensely believed in. Devotion to a woman nobly born, of their own noble race and people, is the theme their poets love to dwell on, and always stands foremost in their scheme of romance. It is the keynote initially struck of every poem of the *Moállakát*. At the same time there is this difference between the devotion of the Arabian lover and that of his imitator in Europe, that the Christian idea of continence as a special virtue does not enter at all into the Arab conception of love; the Bedouin troubadours liked wholly to enjoy their loves. And so too in their rhymes; the cruel and disdainful damsel finds little place in pre-Islamic verse, rather she who has been kind and whom adverse fate has torn away. It is almost always the woman loved and lost that is mourned by them with the most passionate longing, for whom they perform their most glorious deeds, and whom they celebrate in their most enduring songs, the recollection of a short connubial season spent in the enormous solitude of the desert in some shut valley of the desolate hills green for those few sweet weeks of Spring and love, then lost and left unbeautiful for ever.

There is no part of the earth's surface where love exists under such strenuous and endearing conditions as the Arabian desert, where the souls of man and woman are knit so closely by the immense isolation of their lives, where either becomes so dependent on the other by the constant pressure of material dangers. Each little *béyt sháar*, "house of hair," is as a fortress in the wilderness, set up alone in some far valley against the forces of Nature and held there by its dual garrison. In the open plain with its wild, parsimonious beauty, every bush and stone, every beetle and lizard, every rare track of jerboa, gazelle or ostrich on the sand, becomes of value and is remembered, it may be years afterwards, while the stones of the camp-fires stand black and deserted in testimony of the brief season of love. It is only at the time of the *ráhla* or general moving of the camp that the tribe comes together, the men leading their flocks and herds and the women seated, each family in its *hówdaj* or curtained panier, on its tallest camel, and singing as they go. It is always a brilliant spectacle, and one that lives in memory, as the converging lines wind up the valleys at sunrise and over the crests of the hills to their new pastures. This is what Zohéyr so beautifully sings in his poem of the *Moállakát*. His Om-Aufa is the woman he has loved, who has borne him a son, and who is gone. She has left him of her own free will, perhaps by his own fault, perhaps by cruel circumstance, but he shall see her no more. Bedouin romance reaches no higher point than this. The love does not touch him which has been loved in vain. And in truth, love of this sweet domestic kind is not the sole though it is always the leading theme of these wild singers. Mere passion, for pleasure and adventure's sake, is referred to often, and not seldom in boasting terms of favours received or won. The reader of the *Moállakát* must not expect to find in them the refinements of our drawing-room soul-wooers. Neither are the loves of angels in them nor the loves of boys.

Love, however, of any kind, material or ideal, never filled the whole range of vision of the Bedouin singer. More important in his mind are always his dealings with men, and to these he returns as a duty from his excursions in the kingdom of romance. If he boasts occasionally of his love triumphs, ten times more does he boast of his victories in the battlefield, in the council tent, as an entertainer of guests, and even, to his shame, as a wine-bibber. The drinking of wine was considered in pre-Islamic Arabia the test of a generous fancy, and it was no discredit for a young noble to waste his substance in treating his companions to skin after skin of the resin-cured juice of the grape, put up to auction at the wine-seller's, even until all was gone. This, with their love of gambling, is the chief change in manners we find between the ancient Arabia of the *Moállakát* and the modern Arabia where wine and games of chance are wholly unknown. Moral blemishes not a few there are in all the poems, but one would not wish them absent, for they serve to point the reality of the life described. An astonishingly vivid realism is indeed their chief characteristic, and we may well forgive these roystering singers when they tell us of their lapses in view of the splendid pictures they have given us of the sights and sounds and natural wonders of the desert with which they were all familiar. Not even in the Book of Job do we find nobler presentments of four-foot life than in the *Moállakát*. The horse, the camel, the antelope, the wolf, these are over and over again depicted, the wild ass and that most wonderful of created things, the ostrich with its brood. What would we not give for pictures of this naturalistic value in our own ancient poets of the wild ox of Europe, the elk, the beaver and the bear? It was with these living wild creatures that the poets of the Ignorance lived, and it was these that they described, these and the storms which occasionally wrecked their valleys, blotting out in a night the memorial stones of their encampments so touchingly remembered; the sun's heat in their long day marches; the stars hung overhead at night like lamps from the firmament; the ships seen from their sea-coasts; and yet again their camels and their horses, for it was always to these that their thoughts returned, and which they did not weary of depicting or fear to weary their listeners with.

Such was Arabia in the first century before Islam, and such the nature of its poets. Of all that won distinction among them, the most noted were the seven authors of the *Mudáhabát*, "The Golden Odes," known also as the *Moállakát*. The tradition with regard to these is that, at the annual fair held at Okád, in western Nejd, each poet recited a set piece of verse, *Kasída*, it being put to the popular vote to decide upon their merits; and that afterwards those poems which had been judged the best were set down in golden manuscript and hung up in the Káaba at Mecca, and so received the name of the "Golden Odes" or "The Suspended Poems." It is, however, extremely doubtful whether the whole of this story is true. All that is recorded in attestation of it by the early Islamic commentators is contained in a passage of the *Kitáb El Agháni*, the work of the celebrated Abulfáraj of Ispahán, who, writing in the third century of the Hejra, states, on authority he considered valid, that Amr ibn Kolthúm's poem was recited both by himself and by men of his tribe at Okád and at Mecca. There is no word, however, in this narrative, of the poem having been reduced to writing, or of its having been hung up in the Káaba or elsewhere; and what is far more probable is that the story is an attempt by later scholars to find a meaning for the rather obscure titles given to the poems, consonant with modern Mohammedan ideas. As has been well pointed out by Sir Charles Lyall in his exhaustive monograph on the subject, the art of writing was, if not unknown, at least very little practised by the Pagan Arabs, while the allusion to the fine Egyptian linen and the letters of gold, is also somewhat suspicious, as suggesting an epoch when Arabian intercourse with Egypt was closer than in pre-Islamic days.

Be this, however, as it may, the "Seven Golden Odes" or the "Seven Suspended Poems," have come to be considered the classic poems, and have obtained for their authors a special position as the most famous singers of Pagan Arabia. The date of the earliest of them, Imr el Káis', is reckoned to be about the year A.D. 545, and that of the latest, Zohéyr's, about A.D. 605, or within twenty years of the preaching of Islam.

It is a matter of dispute what was the precise effect of the new doctrine on the poetic impulse of Arabia. European writers are generally of opinion that the revelation of the Korán checked, if it did not at once kill, the wild natural growth of song in the Peninsula. They argue that all dogmatic religions, enthusiastically embraced, have a tendency to fill the whole field of passionate imagination to the exclusion of rival passions, and that Islam was fatal to Arabian poetry, just as Christianity had been fatal to the poetry of Greece and Rome. It is certain that the pleasure-loving desert bards were, at least in their praise of lawless love and wine, out of harmony with the austerer thought of Islam. The Liberal school, however, of Mohammedan teaching in our day does not at all admit this statement of the case. It denies altogether that either the Prophet or his immediate successors were hostile to the poets. The two first Caliphs, Abu Békr and 'Omar, are traditionally known to have had the national bards in their intimacy, and it was not till long after, say the 'Ulema, that Arabian poetry began to decline. They hold the verse composed under the

Ommayyád Caliphs to be on a level with the best of pagan times. Nevertheless, it is difficult not to recognize a decay in certain qualities of the later verse which if not due to Mohammedan teaching was at least the result of Islam's triumph in the world. Arabia, within a few years of the Prophet's death, had, like a pent-up flood, overflowed the neighbouring lands, and the outpouring had left the Peninsula depleted of its most vigorous tribes. All that was best of them had passed outside the desert borders and had become city dwellers, in Syria, Irák, Persia and Egypt. Their old ways of thought had been exchanged for new ones; they were no longer Bedouins; they had intermarried with strangers; their insularity was gone. The opinion that good verse was written down to the end of the second century of the Héjra may be, as far as the rules of the art go, a true judgement; but the special desert flavour of the old *Kasídas* is certainly lacking in the new, that splendid realism in regard to natural things, that plainness of speech and that naïveté of passion which distinguish the pre-Islamic work from all other poetry, and which we Europeans find of such priceless value. This was Arabia's loss.

On the other hand, it is quite certain that, but for Islam and the Korán, and their conquest of Persia and the Roman Empire, a fact which made Arabian literature of world-wide importance, not even the small remnant we possess of the pre-Islamic poetry would have been preserved to us. It must be remembered that none of it all, unless we accept the story of the "Suspended Poems," was put down in writing, but had been composed for recitation at the desert gatherings where the poets met and sang. The *Kasídas* passed from mouth to mouth, and as the fresh ones came, the older were gradually forgotten, so that it is extremely improbable that the world at large would ever have heard of them. When, however, Islam had for some generations been firmly established in the neighbouring lands, and especially in Persia and on the Persian frontier, where a taste for literature had long prevailed, a new curiosity sprang up in regard to the language and traditional lore of ancient Arabia. Everything connected with the language of the Korán, now no longer correctly spoken by the Arabs of the emigration, became of religious as well as archaeological importance, and schools were founded whose careful duty it was to collect every scrap of pre-Islamic verse and preserve it, as Europe eight hundred years later set itself to rescue the Greek and Latin Classics. The texts of the various *Kasidas* were thus permanently preserved, and have ever since formed a subject of study, in some sort theological, in the various schools and universities of Islam. And so it was with the *Moallakát*, and is to the present day. This has been the World's gain.

To pass from Asia into Europe, we find the Seven Poems translated first into Latin, and then from Latin into the chief languages of the West during the course of the eighteenth century. The Library of the British Museum contains them under various titles in French, German, Russian and English, the earliest English version being that of Sir William Jones, published in 1782. The present translators, therefore, are unable to claim the honour of putting an unknown work before English scholarship. At the same time, the field they have chosen will, they believe, be found practically virgin by the poetry-reading public. Sir William Jones' translation is a prose one, and its English is of the eighteenth century, polite, latinized, and little suggestive of the wild vigour of the original Arabic. Even so, his version is all but forgotten, though Mr. Clouston included it in 1881 in his Arabian Anthology; nor has any rival translation made its appearance since. Sir Charles Lyall, it is true, made a commencement which promised well in verse, and a single Ode of the Seven was published by him in 1885 in his excellent collection of pieces gathered from the ancient Arabian poets. But the design was not completed, and the *Moállakát*, as a whole, remains a stranger to us still in any form of English verse. The only other translation known to have been made is a word for word rendering in unadorned prose at Bombay by Captain Johnson, which was printed a few years ago for the use of Indian students, an excellent work of its kind, but nothing more.

The present translators, therefore, indulge a hope that the work they have been engaged on will be accepted as an attempt, rather tardy than premature, and altogether needed, to fill a gap in English translated literature. Their aim has been to produce a volume, not for scholars only, but also for all lovers of strange and beautiful verse, such a volume, if possible, as was produced forty years ago by FitzGerald, when he gifted English poetry with the glorious "Quatrains of Omar Khayyám." Their difficulties have been great. The text of the *Moállakát*, in itself obscure, has for centuries been still farther obscured by mediaeval commentators, learned in everything except personal knowledge of the customs and ways of Bedouin thought. Townsmen by birth, this was not to be wondered at, and their mistakes have been handed down from age to age almost as a religion. In dealing with these, the present translators have had the advantage of their long experience of the desert and desert practices, and it may be added, desert politics (for these are essentially the same now in their modern developments as they were in the *Days of the Ignorance*); and they believe that they have been thus able to throw new light on not a few time-honoured obscurities. The text they have followed has been that recently published at Cairo, a text which has been carefully revised by the learned Sheykh el Shangíti, and which has received the imprimatur of the still more learned Grand Mufti, Sheykh Mohammed Abdu. To these great scholars the translators owe a debt of gratitude they here acknowledge in connection with their work, as also to Sheykh Abderrahmán el Aléysh of the Azhar University, and to Abdallah Effendi el Ansári of Cairo. Certain verses, however, of a contested authenticity have, for their intrinsic merit, been added to the accepted version, but in all such cases they will be found so recorded, with the authority on which they rest, in the notes at the end of the volume. None of them are more modern than the second century of Islam.

A far more serious difficulty has been so to simplify and arrange the verses as to make them run easily and intelligibly to English ears. An absolutely verbal rendering of verse in another language is nearly always a betrayal—"*traduttore tradittore*" says justly the Italian proverb—and this is especially true when Arabic and English are in question. To translate baldly, where tongues are so different, is to outrage the original, and often to render it ridiculous. FitzGerald's freehanded method is really the only fair one, and FitzGerald's has been the model taken by the present translators. They have been careful, however, nowhere to violate the text. Each couplet stands self-contained as in the original, and the sense has been always strictly adhered to. Only here and there words have been transposed, and more rarely words added without which no clear meaning could have been conveyed. Those portions especially of the Odes which deal with local events and tribal politics have needed a courageous handling, and the translators hope that the result may have justified them, and that, without referring to the explanatory notes of the Appendix, each poem will now be readable even by those who run. Above all, they hope that their justification will be found in the judgement that what they give is true poetry, a new flower of a strange and interesting kind added to the body of our English classics.

One word may be added, in conclusion, of a technical kind. While the sole responsibility of the verbal rendering has been undertaken by Lady Anne Blunt, that of the verse belongs exclusively to her copartner in the translation. On this half of the work it is necessary to explain that the Arabic metres, which are of extreme brilliancy, have been copied as closely in the English as the difference of the two languages will permit. It has, however, been found impossible to do this absolutely or in all its details. The metrical scheme of the original is based on rules of prosody not unlike those of ancient Greece and has, besides, a terminal repetition peculiar to itself. This is sometimes a rhyming spondee, but more frequently a dactyl with the final syllable repeated at the end of each couplet throughout the poem. It is a form which Arabic, with its extremely regular grammatical inflection, lends itself to naturally, but which in English, or even in Italian, could hardly by any ingenuity be contrived even at the sacrifice of all meaning, in mere nonsense verses. Thus the common form of the Arabic ending would be either such a double rhyme as *hearing*, *cheering*, *endearing*, *interfering*, repeated a hundred times or more with all possible variations, or again such dactyls as *fear of him*, *might of him*, *grieved for him*, *gone with him*. These last it might be possible to prolong in an original poem, but not in a translation where the sense is strictly prescribed and there is almost no imaginative freedom. It has therefore been decided to attempt neither the rhyme nor the terminal syllable, though advantage has been taken of all convenient occasions of conforming to the latter. Thus such expressions in the Odes as *high-set the pass of it*, *blue-black the depths of it*, *dark-crowned the crest of it*, may be accepted as very literal renderings, not only of the sense, but of the form of the original; while in one of the poems the opening couplets, where proper names occur, almost exactly give the rhyming cadence. Apart from this terminal defect, the metres are in close accord with those of the originals, and an attempt has been made by assonances and alliterations in the body of each couplet, still farther to imitate their peculiar sound. The Arabic language is the most accentuated in the world, intended, as has been said of it, to be shouted from hill to hill, and even in its poetry it is possessed of a ring and scansion which any weakness in translation vitiates. At the same time, there are certain changes of accent which, like the half tones in its music, have a subtle effect upon the hearer, more easily recognized than classified. If the English reader, in reciting the "Golden Odes" aloud, feels anything of the thrill of a sudden and unexpected pleasure caused by the cadence, independently perhaps of the meaning, as of something stronger than he is accustomed to, fiercer yet as tender, musical still, while defiant of the common rules of art, the translators' work will not have been done in vain; it will have achieved its full purpose.

Newbuildings Place,
Horsham, Sussex.

June 5, 1903.

FIRST ODE.

IMR-EL-KÁIS.

IMR EL KAIS IBN HEJR is the earliest and most interesting of the Poets of the Ignorance whose work has come down to us. He was of the noblest blood of the Arabs, being descended from the Himyarite Kings of Kíndi, his father, Hejr Ibn El Hárith, being hereditary prince of the two tribes of 'Asad and Ghatafán in Yémen. As the youngest of many sons, Imr-el-Káis was made much of in his father's tent, and as a young man, for his great beauty and wit, by the women of the tribes; and many love adventures are related of him, including those to which he himself refers in his Ode. The scandals caused by these, joined with his inordinate love of poetry, brought down upon him his father's anger, and he was sent away, as young men in disgrace still often are, to herd his father's camels in a distant desert. But this did not last for long, for, neglecting his active duties as herdsman, he spent all his time rhyming about his beasts, and so too with his father's mares, so that lastly, as a supreme disgrace, he was entrusted, as a mere shepherd, with the charge of the sheep. This proved too much for his proud temper, and he refused, and having associated himself with certain bands of young freebooters, *saalík*, he was finally expelled from his father's territories. It was during his wanderings in the years that followed, and when he may have been about twenty-five years of age, that he composed his celebrated Ode, the first of the Moállakát. It was at this time, too, that he married his first wife, not the least light-minded of his adventures, for it is related of him that he had taken a vow never to marry until he should meet a woman who could resolve a riddle he had made, the question of which was "What are two, and four, and eight?" The answer given him had generally been "the number fourteen." But now, as he was travelling in Nejd, he chanced to overtake on the road a certain Sheykh who had with him his daughter, a girl of ready wit, who at once supplied the true solution, as thus: "the two breasts of a woman, the four milking-teats of a she camel, and the eight dugs of a she-wolf." By this wife Imr-el-Káis had several sons and a daughter, Hind.

While wandering thus, news reached him through messengers of his father's death. Hejr had fallen the victim of a revolt of the Béni 'Asad, and before he died had willed the bulk of his flocks and herds, with the duty of vengeance, to whichsoever of his sons on being told of his death should not weep. The elder sons had all shed tears, but Imr-el-Káis was busy draught-playing when the news arrived, and would pay no attention till he had finished and won his game. Then, without sign of grief, he arose, and mounting went back with the messengers, prepared for a deadly revenge. This was what Hejr had intended, and Imr-el-Káis was awarded the inheritance.

The rest of his history, as related by the author of the Kitáb-el-Agháni, which is the chief chronicle and authority on all such matters, is a long narrative of the troubles brought upon him by his filial piety. On his return to Yémen, his kinsmen of Tághleb and Bekr at once espoused his quarrel, and the conjunction struck such terror into the Béni 'Asad, that they sent ambassadors to Imr-el-Káis offering, over and above the usual blood-price, to deliver to him one of their chief men that he might do with him as he would. But Imr-el-Káis, after a night spent in great agitation of mind, in the morning, with tears, refused all compromise, sent the messengers away, and attacked the Béni 'Asad. It happened, however, that these, for more security, had encamped within the lines of another tribe, the Kinána, and as the attack was made before full daylight, the men of Tághleb and Bekr slew without knowing it some of these. With the Kinána they had no quarrel, and they were vexed with Imr-el-Káis for the mistake incurred on his account. Nevertheless they followed on with him on the track of the Béni 'Asad, and came up with them at a certain watering-place and defeated them, but, a part still flying in the night, and Imr-el-Káis still pursuing, Tághleb and Bekr would have no more, and left him with the reproach: "Woe to thee, thou man of evil fortune," and so returned to their homes. Imr-el-Káis on this appealed to others of his kinsmen to take their place, but each in turn refused him help, and it was only with the assistance of mercenaries, broken men of the tribes, that he was able at last to fill his vengeance. It is told of him that having come up, thus accompanied, with the 'Asad at Tebála he turned aside to take an omen, as to his action, of a well-known idol standing there. Following the custom of the pagan Arabs, the form of divination he chose was to cast three arrows on the ground, and according to the way they fell to read a counsel either of attack or of retreat or of waiting a more favourable moment, "the commanding, the forbidding and the postponement," and three times he cast the arrows, and three times they forbade. Then in his anger he gathered the shafts in his hands and broke them across the face of the idol, crying: "Woe to thee, had thine own father been slain, thou wouldst not have hindered me." And he went on and the next day he slew of the enemy the whole count of his blood vengeance, until he was satisfied.

Now the news of these doings came to El Móndir, king of Híra, and he sent horsemen against Imr-el-Káis. And these pressed on Imr-el-Káis and he fled from place to place and from tribe to tribe, from Yémen to Hit on the Euphrates, seeking asylum and carrying with him what remained of his inheritance, and everywhere he was entertained with pleasure on account of his verses, but with fear on account of the King of Híra's anger. And he came in his wanderings to the two hills of Táï, 'Aja and Sélma (which are now Jebel Shammar), and was well received by the Chief of Táï, who gave him a daughter of the tribe Om-Jéndab as second wife. And it is related of this wife that she, too, was a woman of wit, and that one day, being behind the screen listening to her husband and a rival poet, 'Alkama, capping verses in praise of their horses, she was appealed to for a decision of skill between them, and she gave the award to the stranger, her reason being that, whereas Imr-el-Káis had boasted his horse's speed urged on with voice and whip, the boast of the other had been that his horse needed no urging. At this Imr-el-Káis was angered, and on the instant divorced her and travelled onwards, seeking a new resting-place, but pursued always by El Móndir's enmity. In the end, after many wanderings, he found asylum with a certain valorous Jewish chieftain, El Samúeli, who had built for himself a fortress in the oasis of Téyma in Northern Nejd, where he was able to defy all comers. It is related of Imr-el-Káis that he still carried with him five suits of armour inherited from his ancestors, to each of which a name had been given, as long afterwards to their swords by the heroes of Christian chivalry. With him too was his daughter Hind and his cousin Yezíd. These were all received by El Samúeli under his protection, and so remained until, El Móndir still pressing, Imr-el-Káis was unwilling to involve his host in trouble and by his advice went as a suppliant of the *Káisar* to Constantinople.

The position on the Northern frontier, at that time, of Arabia was much what it is now, or rather was a hundred years ago, between the tribes and the Ottoman Empire. The Emperor, without any real power south of Palestine, made always claim to an overlordship of the Peninsula, while on the Eastern side of the desert, the Persian *Kísra*, Chosroes, claimed a like suzerainty over the tribes of the Euphrates through the intermediary of the Kings of Híra. Against Móndir, therefore, the Emperor was a natural protector, and Imr-el-Káis did not appeal in vain. He was passed on by the governors of Palestine and Syria through Asia

Minor to Constantinople, and arrived at the Imperial Court, where he was received with all honour. His rank as a Himyarite prince of the Royal House of Kíndi, gave him admittance to the Emperor's person, and he was lodged in the Palace, just as now the exiled Princes of Nejd who come as suppliants to the Sultan are lodged in Yíldiz. His good fortune, however, did not long continue, and, having been accused of a love-intrigue with the Emperor's daughter, he was forced to embark upon a new journey once more in the direction of his own country. But this he did not live to reach. At 'Angora, as is related, he was overtaken by the Káisar's officers, who, pretending a parting gift from their master, presented him with a robe of honour, poisoned for his destruction. Of it he died, it is said in the year A.D. 565, the forty-fifth of his age. His tomb was still shown to travellers in the second century of the Héjra.

El Samúeli, the Jew, gained high repute among the Arabs for his good faith in connection with this adventure. For, being pressed by the Emperor's vassal, El Hárith, King of Ghassán, to deliver up the five suits of armour which had been left in his charge at Téyma, he refused, although at the cost of his son's life, whom El Hárith had seized as hostage, so that his good faith remained long a proverb among the Arabs.

The metre of Imr el Káis' Ode is what is known as the "long measure," each couplet ending in a double dactyl and the terminal syllable *li*. It is held by Oriental scholars to have been the original model to which all the rest of the Odes more or less closely conformed, and to have founded a new school of verse hitherto unknown in Arabian poetry. Of the whole seven it is the one which has the most of human and natural interest, the least of political invective. It is also the easiest to understand. Apart from the sudden transitions from one subject to another, which are common to them all, there is little that is confusing, or incomprehensible. The poet begins with his own love adventures, realistically told, goes on to describe the night in the desert, and the dawn, the mounting of his horse, the riding down of antelopes and the feast at sunset. The poem ends with the picture of a sudden storm among the hills, a passage which has been rightly judged to be the highest level of poetry reached by the desert singers. It is the earliest and the simplest of the seven Odes, and constructed with the least of conscious art.

THE ODE OF IMR EL KAIS.

WEEP, ah weep love's losing, love's with its dwelling-place
set where the hills divide Dakhúli and Háumali.
Túdiha and Mikrat! There the hearths-stones of her
stand where the South and North winds cross-weave the sand-furrows.
See the white-doe droppings strewn by the wind on them,
black on her floors forsaken, fine-grain of peppercorns.
Here it was I watched her, lading her load-camels,
stood by these thorn-trees weeping tears as of colocynth.
Here my twin-friends waited, called to me camel-borne:
Man! not of grief thou diest. Take thy pain patiently.
Not though tears assuage thee, deem it beseemeth thee
thus for mute stones to wail thee, all thy foes witnesses.
What though fortune flout thee! Thus Om Howéyrith did,
thus did thy Om Rebábi, fooled thee in Másali.
O, where these two tented, sweet was the breath of them,
sweet as of musk their fragrance, sweet as garánfoli.
Mourned I for them long days, wept for the love of them,
tears on my bosom raining, tears on my sword-handle.
Yet, was I un-vanquished. Had I not happiness,
I, at their hands in Dáret, Dáret of Júljuli?

O that day of all days! Slew I my milch-camel,
feasted the maidens gaily,—well did they load for me!
Piled they high the meat-strings. All day they pelted me,
pelted themselves with fatness, fringes of camel-meat.
Climbed I to her howdah, sat with Onéyzata,
while at my raid she chided: Man! Must I walk afoot?
Swayed the howdah wildly, she and I close in it:
there! my beast's back is galled now. Slave of Grief, down with thee.
Answered I: Nay, sweet heart, loosen the rein of him.
Think not to stay my kisses. Here will I harvest them.
Grieve not for thy camel. Grudge not my croup-riding.
Give me—and thee—to taste things sweeter than clove-apples,
Kisses on thy white teeth, teeth, nay the pure petals,
even and clean and close-set, wreathing a camomile.
Wooed have I thy equals, maidens and wedded ones.
Her, the nursling's mother, did I not win to her?

What though he wailed loudly, babe of the amulets,
  turned she not half towards him, half of her clasped to me?
Woe is me, the hard heart! How did she mock at me,
  high on the sand-hill sitting, vowing to leave and go!
Fátma, nay, my own love, though thou wouldst break with me,
  still be thou kind awhile now, leave me not utterly.
Clean art thou mistaken. Love is my malady.
  Ask me the thing thou choosest. Straight will I execute.
If so be thou findest ought in thy lover wrong,
  cast from thy back my garments, moult thee my finery.
Woe is me, the hard heart! When did tears trouble thee
  save for my soul's worse wounding, stricken and near to die?

Fair too was that other, she the veil-hidden one,
  howdahed how close, how guarded! Yet did she welcome me.
Passed I twixt her tent-ropes,—what though her near-of-kin
  lay in the dark to slay me, blood-shedders all of them.
Came I at the mid-night, hour when the Pleiades
  showed as the links of seed-pearls binding the sky's girdle.
Stealing in, I stood there. She had cast off from her
  every robe but one robe, all but her night-garment.
Tenderly she scolded: What is this stratagem?
  Speak, on thine oath, thou mad one. Stark is thy lunacy.
Passed we out together, while she drew after us
  on our twin track to hide it, wise, her embroideries,
Fled beyond the camp-lines. There in security
  dark in the sand we lay down far from the prying eyes.
By her plaits I wooed her, drew her face near to me,
  won to her waist how frail-lined, hers of the ancle-rings.
Fair-faced she—no redness—noble of countenance,
  smooth as of glass her bosom, bare with its necklaces.
Thus are pearls yet virgin, seen through the dark water,
  clear in the sea-depths gleaming, pure, inaccessible.
Coyly she withdraws her, shows us a cheek, a lip,
  she a gazelle of Wújra,—yearling the fawn with her.
Roe-like her throat slender, white as an áriel's,
  sleek to thy lips up-lifted,—pearls are its ornament.
On her shoulders fallen thick lie the locks of her,
  dark as the dark date-clusters hung from the palm-branches.
See the side-plaits pendent, high on the brows of her,
  tressed in a knot, the caught ones fast with the fallen ones.

Slim her waist,—a well-cord scarce has its slenderness.
  Smooth are her legs as reed-stems stripped at a water-head.
The morn through she sleepeth, musk-strewn in indolence,
  hardly at noon hath risen, girded her day dresses.
Soft her touch,—her fingers fluted as water-worms,
  sleek as the snakes of Thóbya, tooth-sticks of 'Ishali.
Lighteneth she night's darkness, ay, as an evening lamp
  hung for a sign of guidance lone on a hermitage.
Who but shall desire her, seeing her standing thus,
  half in her childhood's short frock, half in her woman's robe!
Strip thee of youth's fooling, thou in thy manhood's prime.
  Yet to her love be faithful,—hold it a robe to thee.
Many tongues have spoken, warned me of craft in love.
  Yet have they failed an answer,—all were thine enemies.

Dim the drear night broodeth,—veil upon veil let down,
  dark as a mad sea raging, tempting the heart of me.
Spake I to Night stoutly, while he, a slow camel,
  dragged with his hind-feet halting,—gone the forehand of him.
Night! I cried, thou snail Night, when wilt thou turn to day?
  When? Though in sooth day's dawning worse were than thou to me.
Sluggard Night, what stays thee? Chained hang the stars of thee
  fast to the rocks with hempen ropes set un-moveable.

Water-skins of some folk—ay, with the thong of them
  laid on my nága's wither—borne have I joyfully,
Crossed how lone the rain-ways, bare as an ass-belly;
  near me the wolf, starved gamester, howled to his progeny.
Cried I: Wolf, thou wailest. Surely these lives of ours,
  thine and my own, go empty, robbed of prosperity.
All we won we leave here. Whoso shall follow us,
  seed in our corn-track casting, reap shall he barrenness.

Rode I forth at day-dawn—birds in their nests asleep—
  stout on my steed, the sleek-coat, him the game-vanquisher.
Lo, he chargeth, turneth,—gone is he—all in one,
  like to a rock stream-trundled, hurled from its eminence.
Red-bay he,—his loin-cloth chafing the ribs of him
  Shifts as a rain-stream smoothing stones in a river-bed.
Hard is he,—he snorteth loud in the pride of him,
  fierce as a full pot boiling, bubbling beneath the lid.

Straineth he how stoutly, while, as spent fishes swim,
  tied to his track the fleet ones plough his steps wearily.
See, in scorn he casteth youth from the back of him,
  leaveth the horseman cloakless, naked the hard-rider.
As a sling-stone hand-whirled, so is the might of him,
  loosed from the string that held it, hurled from the spliced ribbon.
Lean his flanks, gazelle-like, legs as the ostrich's;
  he like a strong wolf trotteth; lithe as a fox-cub he.
Stout his frame; behind him, look, you shall note of him
  full-filled the hind-leg gap, tail with no twist in it.
Polished, hard his quarters, smooth as the pounding-stone
  used for a bridegroom's spices, grind-slab of colocynth.
As the henna juice lies dyed on a beard grown hoar,
  so on his neck the blood-stains mark the game down-ridden.
Rushed we on the roe-herd. Sudden, as maids at play
  circling in skirts low-trailing, forth leaped the does of it.
Flashing fled they, jewels, shells set alternately
  on a young gallant's neck-string, his the high pedigreed.
Yet he gained their leaders, far while behind him lay
  bunched in a knot the hindmost, ere they fled scatterwise.
'Twixt the cow and bull herds held he in wrath his road;
  made he of both his booty,—sweatless the neck of him.
All that day we roasted, seethed the sweet meat of them,
  row upon row in cauldrons, firelighters all of us.
Nathless home at night-fall, he in the fore-front still.
  Where is the eye shall bind him? How shall it follow him?
The night through he watcheth, scorneth him down to lay,
  close, while I sleep, still saddled, bridled by side of me.

Friend, thou seest the lightning. Mark where it wavereth,
  gleameth like fingers twisted, clasped in the cloud-rivers.
Like a lamp new-lighted, so is the flash of it,
  trimmed by a hermit nightly pouring oil-sésame.
Stood I long a watcher, twin-friends how dear with me,
  till in Othéyb it faded, ended in Dáriji.
By its path we judged it: rain over Káttan is;
  far in Sitár it falleth, streameth in Yáthboli.
Gathereth gross the flood-head dammed in Kutéyfati.
  Woe to the trees, the branched ones! Woe the kanáhboli!
El Kanáan hath known it, quailed from the lash of it.
  Down from their lairs it driveth hot-foot the ibexes.

Known it too hath Téyma; standeth no palm of her
  there, nor no house low-founded,—none but her rock-buildings.
Stricken stood Thabíra whelmed by the rush of it,
  like an old chief robe-folded, bowed in his striped mantle.
Nay, but he Mujéymir, tall-peaked at dawn of day,
  showed like a spinster's distaff tossed on the flood-water.
Cloud-wrecked lay the valley piled with the load of it,
  high as in sacks the Yemámi heapeth his corn-measures.
Seemed it then the song-birds, wine-drunk at sun-rising,
  loud through the valley shouted, maddened with spiceries,
While the wild beast corpses, grouped like great bulbs up-torn
  cumbered the hollow places, drowned in the night-trouble.

SECOND ODE.

TÁRAFA.

TÁRAFA holds a position with the learned second only to Imr-el-Káis as a pagan poet. This is due less to the verses by him which have been preserved to us, than to a tradition of other verses which have been lost, and to a saying of the commentator Mufáddal, placing him among the masters of the seven long poems which the Arabs call *El Samût*, the "Strings of the Necklace." It is also insisted upon that his Ode is more regular in its composition than any of the Moállakát, a point of criticism which has its full weight in the schools. To the English reader, however, the superiority will be less apparent. It is unquestionable that the opening of Tárafa's Ode is a plagiarism of his great master's Imr-el-Káis; nor does the rest of the poem justify by any special beauty of thought or diction the judgement formed of it. It has been a difficult task to give it a readable English form.

Tárafa, whose real name was Amr Ibn El Abd, was a younger contemporary of Imr-el-Káis, and the youngest in years of all the Arabian poets, dying, it is recorded, at the age of twenty-six. He was of the tribe of Dhóbya, and of the family of its rulers, a wild Bedouin youth—such as may be found not uncommonly at the present day in Arabia—imaginative, impulsive and perverse, embroiled in constant quarrels, hot-tongued and violent-handed. It is related of him that he and his brother Mábad owned a herd of camels between them, and took it in turns to pasture them. But Tárafa was too careless and too fond of verse-making to do his share of the work properly; and this led to a quarrel, which is alluded to in the Ode. For when Mábad reproached him, asking whether, when the camels should have been lost, his poetry could get them back, he answered obstinately that it could, and refused to listen farther. The camels accordingly were one day, as Mábad had predicted, raided and lost. Then Tárafa, to make good his boast, went the round of his relations and friends, asking their help to get back the herd, and among them applied to his cousin Málek, who only reproved him for his idleness and folly, a reproof which, it is said, was the cause of the Ode's being written. It is, however, related that, though no one would help him and the camels were not recovered, Tárafa, nevertheless, was able to perform what he had said, for by his praise in verse he so pleased one of the rich tribe-sheykhs that he obtained from him a hundred camels to replace his own.

His early end came tragically. Having gone to the Court of Amr Ibn Hind, King of Híra, he was sitting one day with the Prince, when the Prince's sister passed by, and Tárafa, though looking away from her, saw her face reflected in the silver cup he was holding in his hand, whereupon in his vanity he recited the following verse:

> "O thou with the roe's neck bending, ear-ringed sweet ring-wearer,
> Had but the king been away, how would thy mouth not have kissed me."

This, coming to Amr's ears, caused much displeasure, and it is said that Tárafa, no longer in favour, made verses against the King, completing thereby the measure of his offence. Amr, however, dissembled his wrath, and sent for Tárafa and another poet, Tárafa's uncle Mutalémmis, who had also offended him; and having loaded them with presents, despatched them on some pretext to Bahréyn on the Persian Gulf, a territory at that time under his rule. And he gave them each a letter to his lieutenant there, as if recommending them.

And Tárafa went out from his presence having no suspicion. But Mutalémmis, being an older man, and of more experience in the ways of Princes, was dissatisfied, and before they had yet left Híra advised that the letters should be opened, that they might see what was written in them. And they found a boy of the inhabitants of Híra, a Christian of the Ebádi, who could understand writing, and Mutalémmis opened his own letter and said to the boy "read what is in this sheet." And the boy read that the King had commanded his lieutenant to slay the bearer. And Mutalémmis threw the letter into the Euphrates and fled. But Tárafa, in his self-confidence, and thinking that Ibn Hind would not dare to deal violently with him, he being as he was of powerful kindred, went on to Bahréyn, and there delivered his missive to the Governor. And the Governor, Robía Ibn El Hárith, being Tárafa's kinsman, sought to save him, and bade him away by night before any should know of his coming. But the boy refused, thinking the other wished to cheat him of a promised reward; and "Walláhi!" he said, "I will not do this thing, and by flight give Amr a pretext against me." So in the morning he was seized and cast into prison. But Robía excused himself with Ibn Hind and would not take his kinsman's life. Then Amr Ibn Hind sent a man of the Bení Tághleb, and set him over Bahréyn in the place of Robía, and he put both Tárafa and Robía to death. And some say that he who actually slew the boy was one Abu Ráshya of the Hawáthir tribe, and that afterwards the tribe paid the blood-wite to the father of Tárafa for his son's death. Accounts differ as to the manner of his punishment. According to some, and they are of most credit, he was slain simply with the sword; according to others he was buried alive, and according to yet others he was allowed to drink wine until he became unconscious, and so had a vein opened in his sleep. Be this as it may, his sister El Khúrnik mourned for him in the following pathetic verses:

"We had counted him but twenty and six of the Spring seasons.
O well had he the years filled, a lord of the strong hand.
We had thought to see him coming, that fair thing, a man to us,
Neither boy nor grey beard,—and here behold him dead."

With regard to the exact date of his Ode, it may be placed about the year B.C. 550, for though some pretend that it was written by him in the last weeks of his life while a prisoner at Bahréyn, internal evidence is much against this. It is clearly the work of a very young man, engrossed with his own small Bedouin troubles and his quarrels with his kinsmen at home. It is far more probable that it was composed in the desert before he had had any experience of Amr ibn Hind's court at Híra. The only lines that at all suggest Bahréyn are those where he compares the howdahs of his tribeswomen to a fleet of ships. But this is far from conclusive. It may be taken as certain that, being the wild youth he was, his anger would have been poured out against Amr, who was actually oppressing him, rather than against his cousin Málek, had it been of the later date.

THE ODE OF TÁRAFA.

THE tent lines these of Kháula in stone-stricken Tháhmadi.
See where the fire has touched them, dyed dark as the hands of her.
'Twas here thy friends consoled thee that day with thee comforting,
cried; not of grief, thou faint-heart! Men die not thus easily.
Ay, here the howdahs passed thee at day-dawn, how royally!
stood for the Dédi pastures;—a white fleet they seemed to thee,
Ships tall-rigged from Adáuli—of Yámin the build of them—
wandering wide the night through, to meet at the sun-rising.
Thus climbed they the long wave-lines, their prows set how loftily!
ploughing the drifted ridges, sand heaped by the sand-seers.

Alas for the dark-lipped one, the maid of the topazes,
hardly yet grown a woman, sweet fruit-picking loiterer!
A girl, a fawn still fawnless, which browses the thorn-bushes,
close to the doe-herd feeding, aloof in the long valleys.
I see her mouth-slit smiling, her teeth,—nay, a camomile
white on the white sand blooming and moist with the night-showers.
Sun-steeped it is, pure argent, white all but the lips of her,
these are too darkly painted to shrink from the sun-burning.
The face of her how joyous, the day's robe enfolding her,
clean as a thing fresh fashioned, untouched by sad time-fingers.

Enough! New joys now claim me. Ay, mount and away from her!
Here on my swift-foot camel I laugh at love's bitterness.
Ship-strong is she, my naga, my stout-timbered road-goer,
footing the long-lined path-way—a striped cloak—in front of us.
Steel tempered are her sinews. She runs like an ostrich-hen,
one which has fled defying the ash-plumed proud lord of her.
Out-paces she the best-born, shank still on shank following,
threading the mazes lightly. Ah, what foot shall follow her?
The spring-long on Kufféyn she has wandered, her kind with her,
pastured in pleasant places, the rain-watered thyme-valleys,
Has turned to her herd's calling, aloft in wrath brandishing,
scared by the thick-furred red thief, that proud tuft the tail of her.
Her tail sways this and that way—a falcon, the wings of him
bating her flanks impatient—erect stands the bone of it—
So lasheth she in anger anon her croup-rider's knee,
then her own shrunken udder, a drought-withered water-skin.
Note well her limbs' perfection, her thighs like the elbow-worn
jambs of a city gateway, two smooth shafts of porphyry.

Her barrel—a stone well-mouth, like bent bows the curves of it,
  cave where the neck-shaft enters, ends in an arched hollow.
Deep dens are her two arm-pits, a tree-trunk with cavities.
  Bows are her rib-bones bended, her spine the hands holding them.
Her elbows are twin buckets, the pails of a water-man
  wide-set, the neck between them the strong man who carries them.
Bridge-like, and Roman-builded! How swore he its architect
  none should leave work or loiter, its key-stone unlaid by them!
Red chestnut is her chin-tuft, a vast vault the back of her.
  Swift-step her hind-feet follow the path of her fore-footing.
Her legs are a cord twisted. Towards them the arms of her
  slant from the shoulders outward, a tent-roof the slope of them.
So sways she, the strong-skulled one, and lightly her shoulder blades
  rise from her spine alternate, arhyme with the march of her.
Like rain-pools in the smooth rock, so, flecking the sides of her,
  white stand the girth-marks, witness once of the sores on them.
Her neck, how tall, how proud-set! Behold her! She raises it
  high as in ships of Díjleh the point of a stern-rudder.
Her head-piece a stout anvil, and, joined to it hardily
  sharp as a file the neck-ridge, fixed as a vice to it.
Her jowl a Syrian parchment, clean vellum the lip of her,
  smooth as a hide of Yémen, no skin-crease nor fold in it.
Her eyes two mirrors shining, her bent brows the shade of them,
  pitted with deep-set hollows, as rock-holes for rain-water.
Eyes dark-rimmed, pure of dust-stains. You gaze in the depths of them
  as in a wild cow's wide eyes, scared for the calf of her.
Ears fearful of the night-sounds, the whispers, the murmurings
  caught in the darkness passing—night—day—they can rest never.
Their thorn-tips tell her lineage, a wild bull's of Háumala
  raging alone forsaken; her breeding you read in them.
Heart watchful of strange dangers, yet stout in the face of them.
  Firm as a test-stone standing where cleft lie the base pebbles.
Lip slit, nose pierced for nose-ring, how slender its cartilage!
  Nobly she lowers it running and stretched to the front of her.
I strike at her my nága: I force her: I hurry her,
  while in our path the false-lights lure us to follow them.
The gait of her how rhythmic! She sways like a dancing-girl,
  one with the white skirts trailing, who bends to the lord of her.
Obedient to your riding, she slackens her outrunning,
  watches the hide-thong twisted, the speed that you need of her.

Her head by your hand close held, your knee-crutch how near to it!
  Then with her fore arms swimming, an ostrich, she flies with you.

Thus rode I, and thus spake he, the friend of my tear-sheddings:
  O for the wit to cure thee, but and my own sorrows!
His soul within him trembled; it seemed to his hardihood
  death and a sure destruction, though far we from road-farers.
For which of us is valiant? When men speak of true valour,
  I feel my own the name named. Straight am I roused by it.
No recreant I, my tent-ridge I hide from no enemy.
  Nor in the far hills build it who bring men a swift succour.
The hand that seeks shall find me. I stand at the gatherings.
  Ay, where men tap the wine-skin, 'tis there they shall speak with me.
What day the tribes assemble, behold me conspicuous,
  sitting as fits my lineage, nor go I in fear of them.
Beside me my companions, bright stars of nobility.
  Dyed is her robe with saffron the girl who pours out to us.
O sweet is her shirt's neck-slit, set wide to the eyes of us.
  Soft is the thing it hides there. We bade her: Now, sing to us.
Ay sing to us: we prayed her. And she, with monotony
  striking a low note slowly, chaunted unchangingly.
O strange it was that cadence: it came back the wail of it,
  grave as a mother's grieving the one son new-slain from her.

Thus sang she. And I spared not the full cups of revelry,
  not till my spoil was wasted, my whole wealth's inheritance.
Then left me they that loved me. Then shunned me my tribe-fellows.
  Sat I alone forsaken, a mange-stricken male camel.
Nathless the poor showed pity, the sons of Earth's particles,
  these and the alien tent-lords, the far chiefs befriended me.
You only did revile me. Yet, say, ye philosophers,
  was that same wealth eternal I squandered in feasting you?
Could all you my fate hinder? Friends, run we ahead of it,
  rather our lives enjoying, since Time will not wait for us.
And, truly, but for three things in youth's day of vanity,
  fain would I see them round me the friends at my death-bedding,
As first: to outstrip the sour ones, be first at the wine-bibbing,
  ay, at the blink of day-dawn when mixed the cup foams for me;
And next, to ride their champion, who none have to succour them,
  fierce on my steed, the led one, a wolf roused and thirst-stricken;

And third, to lie the day-long, while wild clouds are wildering,
  close in her tent of goat's hair, the dearest beloved of me.
O noble she, a tree-stem unpruned in her maidenhood,
  tall as a branch of Khírwa, where men hang their ornaments.
'Tis thus I slake my soul's rage, the life-thirst so wild in me.
  If we two died to-morrow, think, which would go thirstier?
For lo, his grave the miser's! Lo, next it the prodigal's!
  Both are alike, scant favour to hoarder or squanderer.
'Neath mounds of earth the twain lie, a low stone atop of them,
  heavy and broad and shapeless, with new slabs o'erlaying it.
Death is no subtle chooser. He takes all, the free-givers,
  ay, and the rogues close-fisted, the fast-handed gold-hiders.
And life's heap lies unguarded. The night-thieves make spoil of it.
  All that these leave the day-thieves straightway come plundering.
Nay, by thy life—I swear it, though fast fly the heels of him,
  Death has a lead-rope round him, loose though it seem to you.

Ha! How is this? My kinsman? my fool-cousin Máleki?
  Daily, as I draw near him, he turns his mad back on me.
He frowns I know not wherefore. He flouts me, as once with them
  Kurt, in the face of all men, flouted and jibed at me.
His help he has denied me; and, truly, our brotherhood
  tried in the fire of asking lies dead in love's sepulchre.
My word his words discredit. Yet all I for Mábadi
  asked was a poor assistance to gather his lost camels,
I who hold fast to kinship. I swear by the luck of thee,
  when they shall want hard riding, that day they shall fawn on me,
What day their tribes need succour, when loudly their womenfolk
  cry from his hand the oppressor's to hands that are mightier.
Be but their honour tainted, I straight will pour out for them
  death as from brimming cisterns, nor ask for an argument.
They rail at and revile me, who know me no ill-doer;
  me, who have borne their burdens, cast would they out from them.
Yet, had my friend been other, this Málek of larger soul,
  long had my pain been ended, a respiting found for me.
Shame on him for his baseness. His black hand would strangle me,
  whether I thanked or sued him, or turned but my back on him.
O cruel is the sword-stroke: it bites with an Indian edge:
  yet is their temper keener, the clowns I call kin to me.
Then leave me to my own ways, my tent set in Dárghadi,
  far from the eyes of all men, and earn thee my gratitude.

TÁRAFA

Had he, the Lord, so willed it, my name had been Khâlidi,
  or had he willed it Ámer, or Kâis, or Mârthadi.
Wealth had been mine and increase, ay, all that men most covet,
  sons as a gift of heaven, a proud-lined posterity.
Yet see me a man subtle, one lithe-souled and lithe-bodied,
  quick as a snake for wounding, whose head is a hurt to them.
The oath my tongue has sworn to is this, to keep close to me
  ever my sword-blade loosened; of Indies the edge of it.
Such blade, if I take vengeance and rise up and smite with it,
  needs not a second down-stroke; I wield me no wood-chopper.
My sword is my true brother. It grudges no blood-spilling.
  Called on to spare, it answers: My lord alone holdeth me.
Thus was I when men armed them and rushed to the battle-field:
  grasped I my sword-hilt foremost, nor feared what fate doomed for me.

Herds knelt, their necks stretched earth-long. How scared them the eyes of me,
  me with my sword drawn marching, its sheath cast away from me.
There passed a strong fair nâga, a full-uddered milch-camel,
  joy of her lord, the gray-beard, a hot man, though time-troubled.
He shouted when she fell there, her stout sinews houghed by me:
  Man, art thou blind who seest not thy sword hath done robbery?
He spake, and to his friends turned: Behold him, this wine-bibber!
  What is his rage against us, his wild words, his drink-folly?
Yet paused: Nay, give him wide room and leave it to profit him:
  herd we the scared ones rather, lest more he should slay of them.
Then fell the maids aroasting its fair flesh the foal of her,
  nor of the fat denied us, the whole hump our prize of it.
We cast the arrows gaily, the dun shafts, the fire-hardened:
  each time the holder held them, straightway I won with them.

When I am dead, speak kindly, thou daughter of Mâbadi:
  rend for my sake thy garments as one worth the love of thee.
Nor count me with the lewd folk, the night-knaves, the roysterers,
  men with nor wit nor wisdom nor will to do weightily,
Men slow to deeds of virtue, men swift but in ill-doing,
  men by the brave held lightly, with spread palms and brow-knitting.
For, had I been a weakling, know well, their mad hate of me
  long had been my destruction, their blind wrath my butchery.
Only it wards me from them the fear of my hand's valour,
  this, and my faith untainted, my fame too of ancestry.

Once on a time I bound me with vows, on the battlefield
ever to guard the weak posts, points where the foe threatened,
Points where the bravest faltered, where pale men stood panic-struck,
where they the strong-hearts trembled, faint through the fear in them.
Nay, by thy life, I fear not. I hold not time weariness;
neither hath day distressed me, nor night what it brought to me.
Because I see Death spares none. It smites with an even hand,
bows not to names exalted, nor knows it men's dignities;
Because with Death behind me, myflight can avail me not,
neither can I outwit him, he lying in wait for me.
Because if one be proved vain by those who seek aid of him,
helpless to hurt the harmful, better he perished.
The days to come, what are they? A handful, a borrowing:
vain is the thing thou fearest. To-day is the life of thee.
And death is as a well-spring; to it men pass and pass:
near them is each to-morrow; near them was yesterday.
Only shall Age, the slow-foot, arraign thee of ignorance:
only shall One bring tidings, when least thou desirest him,
One who is hard to deal with, of whom thou art ransomer
neither for pay nor raiment, nor madest thou tryst with him.

THIRD ODE.

ZOHÉYR.

THE character of Zohéyr stands in strong contrast with that of the two poets his immediate predecessors. Both Imr-el-Káis and Tárafa were men of wild, ill-regulated lives, who in the midst of their excesses were cut off young by violent deaths, whereas Zohéyr lived on to extreme old age, respected by all, wise, virtuous and self-contained. Their contemporary by birth, he nevertheless belongs almost to the days of Islám, for it is reported of him that at the age of ninety he was brought into the Prophet's presence, and was recognized by him as the greatest of the poets. Mohámmed indeed is said to have exclaimed on seeing him: "God keep me from his Spirit!" a saying on which is founded the teaching of certain Moslem theologians that, just as the prophet was inspired by an angel with the verses of the Korán, so the Poets of the Ignorance had each his familiar, a spirit of evil, who whispered in his ear the lines he uttered. The belief is not very different from that of the early Christians, who affirmed of the pagan Oracles that they were the voices of demons speaking through the priestesses,—"Oracula gentium daemonia." It is added that after the Prophet's admonition Zohéyr made no more verses. The Caliph 'Omar, too, is reported to have said of Zohéyr that he was the Poet of Poets, "a lord of great wealth, wise, and even in the days of the Ignorance a man of known piety."

Zohéyr Ibn 'Abi Súlma was of the tribe of Mazína, and connected in blood through his father's mother to that of Mórra, both tribes being of Hejáz. Of Zohéyr's father, 'Abu Súlma, it is told that he went out with his Mórra kinsmen, Asáad and Káab, on a raid against Táï, and that having driven home a large booty of camels, he claimed of them his share, but Asáad refused. And Abu Súlma refrained till night-time. But, when it was dark, he sought his mother from among the Mórra, and threatened her, saying: "By him by whom I swear, arise and mount or I will strike thee beneath the earrings with this sword." And she went to the captured camels and seized one by the hump and mounted. And Abu Súlma drove them before him from the Mórra tents, until he came to his own people. And it fell out not long after, that he joined the Mazína on a foray against the Beni Dobián, a sept of Mórra, and when they had arrived over against the Ghatafán, who were neighbours to the Mórra, the Mazína raiders turned back in fear, leaving him alone. And Abu Súlma, once more angry, went down to the tents of Ghatafán and dwelt with them. Thus it happened that Zohéyr spent his childhood with these, and not with his own people; and he makes allusion to such dwelling among strangers when he sings:

"That he who fleeth his kin shall fare far, foes for his guest-fellows."

Zoheyr is known to have been twice married, first to Om 'Aufa, the love of his youth, of whom he so touchingly sings in his Kasída; and secondly to the mother of his two sons, Káab and Bujéyr. Om 'Aufa's sons had died, and so he had taken this other to wife. But Om 'Aufa would not forgive him his second marriage, and for some wrong she did him he put her away, though afterwards bitterly repenting. And it is for this he mourns.

Ibn el Arábi narrates of Zohéyr that he had a son named Sálim, who was of such surprising beauty, and with such a wealth of hair, that a woman of the Arabs, who once saw him as he was riding by, clothed in two striped cloaks at the water of Natáh, exclaimed, "Never beheld I yet the like of this day, nor the like of this man, nor the like of these cloaks, nor such a horse." And the horse suddenly stumbled and fell, and the horse's neck was broken and the neck of his rider.

Ibn el Arábi also records that Zohéyr's father was a poet, and his mother's brother and his sister, Súlma, and his two sons were poets, and his sister El Khansáu was a poet, and his son's son El Módrib Ibn Káab. When his uncle Basháma was dying, he divided his wealth among those of his kin, but to Zohéyr, though he loved him, he gave nothing. "What then," said Zohéyr, "is there no portion left for me?" "Nay," said the old man, "I leave thee the best of all, my wit to make verse." "It was already from the beginning mine," said Zohéyr. But Báshama answered, "That is not so. The sons of the Arabs know well that it passed from me to thee."

And the occasion of the making of his Ode is thus related in the Kitáb el Aghâni:

There was a certain great lord of Dobián, El Hárith Ibn Auf; and he asked one day of his kinsman Khárijeh, boasting: "Who is there among the sons of the Arabs who would deny me his daughter to wife?" And Khárijeh said: "Aus Ibn Háritheh of Táï would deny thee." So El Hárith called to his servant and bade him "mount with me." And they rode until they came to Aus in the land of Táï. And when Aus saw El Hárith, he greeted him, and asked what brought him. "I have come a wooing," said he. And Aus: "This is no place for thy wooing." And he turned his back on him. And Aus' wife reproved him for what he had done, saying: "Dost thou then wish thy daughters to remain unwedded? This is El Hárith Ibn Auf of Mórra, a great lord of the Arabs. Go after him and entreat him and bring him back with thee, and say thou foundest me in anger because of thy sudden proposals, but now return I pray thee and all shall be as thou desirest." And Aus followed after El Hárith. And he who told the tale says: "By God, I was journeying on our way and I chanced to raise my eyes and I saw Aus riding after us. And I called to El Hárith, but he answered nothing by reason of his anger. And I said: 'Here is Aus Ibn Háritheh following after us.' And he answered: 'What have we to do with Aus? Pass on.' And Aus called to us: 'O Hárith! Wait a while for me.' So we waited, and he spoke to us as his wife had bade him. And El Hárith went back with him gladly. And Aus called his eldest daughter to him and said to her: 'This is Hárith Ibn Auf, lord of the Arabs, who asketh that I should give him a daughter to wife. What sayest thou?' And she answered: 'Do it not.' And he asked her 'Why?' And she said: 'I am a woman ill-favoured in my face and sudden in my temper. I am not his uncle's daughter that he should regard our kinship, nor is he thy neighbour in the land that he should fear thee. I am in dread lest he one day should find me displeasing, and should put me from him, and it should happen to me as it is wont to happen in marriage.' And he said 'God bless thee! Call me another.' And he named his second daughter. But she spoke as her sister had spoken: 'I am unskilful with my hands. I fear lest he should put me away.' And he said, 'Call me Buhéyseh.' And she was his youngest daughter, and she stood before him and answered: 'I am fair of face and skilful with my hands, of nature noble and honoured in my father. If Hárith should put me from him, the ill-fortune would be his own.' And he said 'God bless thee.' Then he came out to us and said: 'I wed to thee, O Hárith, Buhéyseh daughter of Aus.' And Harith said 'I take her.' And Aus bade her mother make ready the wedding, and he built a tent for El Hárith. And when the girl was dressed and arrayed, he sent her in to El Hárith. But El Hárith was with her but a little while, and presently came forth. And I questioned him: 'How has it fared with thee? Hast thou prospered?' And he answered: 'No.' And I asked him what had befallen. And he said: 'When I put forth my hand to her, she stopped me, saying: "Wouldst thou do thus with me in the presence of my father and my brethren? Walláhi! It were unseemly."' Then he commanded that they should make ready the camels, and we mounted, taking Buhéyseh with us on our way. And when we had journeyed a short stage, El Hárith bade me ride ahead of them. And he turned aside with her from the road. And presently he joined me, and I asked: 'Hast thou prospered?' And he made answer: 'No. For she said to me: "Wouldst thou do with me as with a slave, a woman taken in battle? By God! not until thou hast slain the camels and slaughtered the sheep and called all the Arabs to the feasting and done for me all that should be done for one of my dignity."' And I approved her and said: 'She is a woman of courage and understanding. She shall be a fitting wife to thee and shall bear thee glorious sons.' And we travelled on until we came to our own pastures. And El Hárith made ready the camels and the sheep and prepared a feast. Then he went in to her. And in a little while he came forth, and again I questioned him: 'Hast thou prospered?' And again he said: 'No. For when I went in to her and said, "Lo, I have made ready the camels and the sheep as thou seest," she made answer "I was told that thou hadst in thee a nobility which I do not see in thee. And truly thou hast a light heart to wed women when the sons of the Arabs are slaying one another." And I asked her what she would have me do. And she answered: "Go forth to them thy kindred and make peace between them; then return to thy wife and thou shalt not lack the thing thou desirest."' And I said, 'Truly a wise and noble woman. She hath spoken a goodly word.' And he said 'Come forth with me.' So we went forth and came to the two tribes (Abs and Dobián), and stood as peacemakers between them. And the peace was made on the agreement that the slain should be counted and the price of the excess paid by the tribe which had slain the more. And we two bore the burden of the blood-wite. And the reckoning was three thousand camels, and these we delivered over in the space of three years. And we came back home with a fair name. And El Hárith went in to his wife, and she bore him sons and daughters."

But, while Abs and Dobián were yet treating for the peace and the tents of both were pitched together, a man of Dobián, Huséyn Ibn Démdem, whose father and brother had been slain in the war by men of the house of Ghálеb of Abs, and who had sworn an oath that he would not wash his head until he had slain one of the house of Ghálеb, chanced to be among them. And a man of Abs came unwitting to his tent, and Huséyn questioned him closely as to his house and lineage, and, learning that he was of Ghálеb, slew him. And the news came to El Hárith and Hárim, and it was grievous to them. And it came also to the men of Abs; and they mounted and rode to El Hárith's tent to slay him, for El Hárith was akin to Huséyn Ibn Dém-dem. And El Hárith sent to meet them a hundred camels, and with them his son, and he said to the messenger: "Say to them, 'are the camels dearer to you or are your lives dearer?'" And El Rábi, the leader of Abs, called aloud to his people: "O men! Your brother has sent you this message." And they said: "we will take the camels." So peace again was made. And El Hárith and Hárim gained the more praise.

It is of this deed of the two peace-makers that Zohéyr sings in his Ode. The Ode would seem to have been written, at least the latter part of it, in extreme old age, and its maxims epitomise all the wisdom of Bedouin maturity still current in the desert. The metre of the poem is the same "long measure" as that of the two first Odes, but with certain varieties of accentuation which it has been sought to reproduce.

THE ODE OF ZOHEYR.

WOE is me for 'Ommi 'Aufa! woe for the tents of her
lost on thy stony plain, Durráj, on thine, Mutethéllemi!
In Rákmatéyn I found our dwelling, faint lines how desolate,
tent-marks traced like the vein-tracings blue on the wrists of her.
Large-eyed there the wild-kine pastured, white roes how fearlessly,
leaped, their fawns beside them, startled—I in the midst of them.
Twenty years abroad I wander. Lo, here I stand to-day,
hardly know the remembered places, seek I how painfully.
Here our hearth-stones stand, ay, blackened still with her cooking-pots,
here our tent-trench squarely graven, grooved here our camel-trough.
Love, when my eyes behold thy dwelling, to it I call aloud:
Blessed be thou, O house of pleasure, greeting and joy to thee!

Friend of my soul! Dost thou behold them? Say, are there maidens there,
camel-borne, high in their howdahs, over the Júrthum spring?
Say, are their curtains lined with scarlet, sanguine embroideries,
veiling them from eyes of all men, rose-tinted coverings?
Slantwise up El Subáan they mounted—high-set the pass of it.
With them the new-born morning's beauty, fair-faced and fortunate.
At the blink of dawn they rose and laded. Now, ere the sun is up,
point they far to Wády Ras, straight as hand points to mouth.
Joy! Sweet joy of joys! Fair visions, human in tenderness,
dear to the human eye that truly sees them and understands!
As the scarlet fringe of fénna seed-pods no lip hath browsed upon,
so is the dye of their scarlet wool new-fringing the camping-grounds.
And they came to the watering pool in the red rocks—blue-black the depths of it.
And they planted the tent-poles, straight and fairly, firm for a dwelling-place.
They have left Kanáan on the far right hand—dark-crowned the crest of it.
How many foes in El Kanáan! And friends, too, ah, how many!
But they came to El Subáan in their might, impetuous, beautiful,
they in their howdahs of scarlet wool. O friend, dost thou look on them?

I have sworn by the most illustrious dwelling, shrine of processioners,
house revered of Koréysh and Júrhum, founded in piety.
I have sworn my praise to the two chieftains, men of what hardihood,
prompt to do when need shall call them, light deeds and doughty deeds.
Strove ye well, ye Lords of Mórra, what though the clans of you
long had drowned in blood their friendship, drowned it in war-clamours.

Ye with Abs and Dóbián that day ye persuaded them,
spite of feud and their death-dealing perfumes of mínshami.
For thus ye spake: Let peace be garnered, all the fair wealth of it,
based on pay and fair exchanges, ours to establish it.
Theirs the peace and yours the glory, high names and dignities,
you the noble twain prevailing, purging the rage of them.
Lo, in Maád ye stand exalted, ye the high-guided ones.
He who a booty brings of glory, shall he not share in it?
Healing of wounds ye dealed in hundreds, hundreds of debt-camels,
guiltless you for the death-guilty, ending the feud of them.
Tribe and tribe, you paid the ransom, what though the hands of you
clean were of blood and the red shedding, ay, the least cup of it.
Yet ye brought the payment bravely, all your fair heritage,
camels yours by right of plunder, these and your ear-marked ones.

Ho! to the oath-bound tribes a greeting: Have ye not sworn to it?
Ay, and to Dóbián a message: Will ye not keep the peace?
For you may not hide from God your dealings, what though in secrecy
deep in your heart of hearts you seal it. Nathless He knoweth it,
Knoweth and taketh note in patience, sure of His reckoning
till the day of the great counting, waiteth or hasteneth.
War! Ye have learned it all, its teachings, well have ye tasted them.
These no tales are that I tell you. Each is a certainty.
A smouldering coal ye flung it lightly, blindly despising it.
Lo, into raging flame it leapeth, wind-lit, destroyeth you.
Ye are ground as corn by Hate's ill-grinding, flat on her grinding-skin.
Nay, a too fruitful camel she. Twins hath she borne to you,
Sinister sons of fear and anger, milk-fed on bitterness;
dark as his, Aád's, their nursing. Lo, she is weaned of them.
And her hand is large to rain you harvests, evil the wealth of them.
No such plenty Irák hath garnered, hell-grain and hate-money.

Ay, by my life, the kin was noble. Yet did it fare with them
ill when they the peace-terms flouted. Démdem's the sin of it,
His, Huséyn's, who held his counsel, hiding the thought in him,
yielding naught and naught revealing, steeled in his stubbornness.
For he thought: My end will I accomplish. No ill shall come to me,
fenced and armed, with might behind me, warriors, horse-riders.
Proud he stood, nor feared the tent-lords, what though Om-Káshami
watched them near, the vulture-mother, eyeing the multitude.
Strode he forth, full-armed, a wild beast, fierce for the blood-letting,
mane and claws unclipped, a lion. Who shall his anger brave?

Fearless, one who doth his vengeance swift on his wrong-doer,
one who unassailed yet rendeth, he the first injurer.
And they pastured there their fair milch-camels, drove to the waterings,
drank of the full pools brimming over, gall in the hearts of them,
This side and that by blood divided, rank hate the meat of them,
poison-grass to their herds' hurting, mired in blood-bitterness.
Yet, by thy life, not these the guilty. Clean was the steel of them,
pure of blood, Nahík's. They slew not him nor Muthéllemi,
Shareless sharers of the death-due. No blood of Náufali
stood to their account, nor Wáhab's, nay, nor Mukházzemi's.
Blameless! Clean! Yet have I seen them drive to the ransoming
camel-herds untouched, unblemished, fresh from the rock-valleys.
Succour to the tribe that succoured! Who but shall haste to them
in their night of fear, of blackness! All men shall speed to them,
Since they gave, since them the avenger gained not to ill-willing,
nay, nor suppliant failed of favour. Him they abandoned not.

I am weary of life who bear its burdens fourscore and how many
years of glory and grief counted. Well may he weary be,
I know to-day, the day before it, ay, and the days that were,
yet of to-morrow I know nothing. Blind are the eyes of me.
I have seen Fate strike out in the darkness, strike like a blind camel:
some it touched died straight, some lingered on to decrepitude.
I have learned that he who giveth nothing, deaf to his friends' begging,
loosed shall be to the world's tooth-strokes: fools' feet shall tread on him;
That he that doeth for his name's sake fair deeds shall further it,
but he that of men's praise is careless dwindleth in dignity;
That he, the lord of wealth, who spendeth naught of his heaped money,
him his kinsfolk shall hold lightly: children shall mouth at him;
That he who keepeth faith shall find faith; who in simplicity
shall pursue the ways accustomed, no tongue shall wag at him;
That he who flieth his fate shall meet it, not, though a sky-ladder
he should climb, shall his fear fend him: dark death shall noose him down;
That he who gifteth the unworthy, spendthrift through idleness,
praised shall be to his dispraising, shamed at his fool-doing;
That he, who shall refuse the lance-butts borne by the peace-bearers,
him the lance-heads shall find fenceless, naked the flesh of him;
That he who guardeth not his tent-floor, with the whole might of him,
cold shall be his hearth-stone broken, ay, though he smote at none;
That he who fleeth his kin shall fare far, foes for his guest-fellows;
that he who his own face befouleth none else shall honour him;

That he, who casteth not the burdens laid on the back of him,
  sheer disgrace shall be his portion, waged as he merited;
That whatso a man hath by nature, wit-wealth or vanity,
  hidden deep, the day shall prove it: all shall be manifest.
For how many sat wise while silent, yet was their foolishness
  proved when their too much, too little, slid through their mouth-slitting.
The tongue is the strong man's half; the other half is the heart of him:
  all the rest is a brute semblance, rank corporality.
Truly, folly in the old is grievous; no cure is known for it:
  yet may the young their soul's unwisdom win to new sanity.

We asked once, and you gave a guerdon,—twice and again you gave:
  only the mouth that hath no silence endeth in emptiness.

FOURTH ODE.

LEBÍD

LEBÍD IBN RABÍA of the Béni Keláb lived also from the days of the Ignorance to those of Islám, and in extreme old age embraced the new faith and renounced the exercise of his art for ever. It is a pious legend that his conversion came about in this way: 'Arbed, Lebíd's half-brother, having come to Mohámmed with a deputation from the Keláb, with the intention, as some say, of treacherously killing the prophet, and for some words of impiety uttered by him, was struck by lightning and perished. Thereupon a second deputation sought the prophet, and among them Lebíd. And being at Mecca he affixed to the gate of the Káaba a poem which he had made, and which runs thus:

> "Yea, all that is is vain, save One, the lord of all.
> and all sweet things deceive: they fail and flee and fade.
> And Man! What griefs shall be, what fears on him forlorn,
> what paleness in that hour, pale, to his fingers pale!
> And each sad mother's son, though he out-run the term,
> time's utmost count of years, to earth shall yield him soon.
> And every Soul in pain its labour's worth shall learn,
> its wage of weal and woe, on that last day of doom."

All the people of Mecca were in admiration at these verses, and no man ventured to recite in rivalry with them. But after a while there was found a new poem written beside it, and this was the famous Second Chapter of the Korán, which when Lebíd saw and learned that it had been set there by Mohámmed, the old poet made his obeisance to the younger, and recognized him as the Prophet of God.

This tale, though cherished by the devout, is not held to be authentic history, and is in itself improbable. All that is certain is that at a very advanced age, it is said a hundred years, Lebíd professed Islám, and that he lived on held in high honour until the days of the Caliph Moáwiyah.

Although the tradition of Lebíd's sayings in his later days as a Moslem is very copious, almost nothing has been recorded of his pagan youth, perhaps because he himself wished it forgotten. The only story which is of any interest for us regarding it, is that when still almost a boy he travelled with certain of the Beni Jáfar, his branch of the Keláb, to the Court of Naamán, King of Híra, and that, while the others went into the Palace he, as the youngest, was left outside to guard their camels. And when they returned he saw that they were troubled, and he besought them to say what had befallen them. And when he pressed them they told him that they had been ill-received through the bitter tongue of one El Rábi, a poet of the tribe of Abs their enemy, whom they had found sitting with the King. And they knew not how to be revenged on El Rábi. And Lebíd said: "Take me with you to-morrow and I will confound him in verse." And they said "Who art thou that thou shouldest find a thing to say?" And he bade them make trial of him. And there was in front of them a low shrub of poor aspect and scanty of foliage, its name *táriba*. And they said, "make essay of thy mockery on her." And he recited in rhythm:

> "This is that táriba,
> Feedeth no fire-flame

Delighteth no dwelling,
Greeteth no neighbour,
Wood of her meagre,
Branch of her brittle,
Worth of her nothing,
Worst herb of pasture,
Lightest of leafage,
Rudest to root up,
Home the remotest,
Her eater shall hunger."

And they said to one another: "We will wait till the morning, and then we will answer him." And Amr, Lebid's cousin, who was the chief of them, said, "We will watch the boy, and if we see him sleeping through the night be assured he is no proper match for El Rábi. But, if he keepeth vigil, he may profit us." And they watched him, and he remained seated till morning on a *shedád* or camel saddle, clutching its pummel with his teeth. And so he remained till dawn. And at dawn they said to him "Thou art our man." And they took him with them to Naamán. And El Rábi made jests at them as before in verse. But the boy confounded him with his replies till in shame El Rábi fled out of Naamán's presence, and Naamán would see him no more.

The Ode of Lebíd would seem to have been made by him soon after this. It contains very direct allusions to what had happened at Híra, and its youthfulness of tone marks it as an early utterance of his Bedouin days. In all the Moállakát there is perhaps nothing more beautiful than his description of the *bákar wáhash* or Oryx antelope, a purely desert animal found only in the Nefúds. This alone proves him to have been from his boyhood a true desert dweller.

In this Ode, as in Zohéyr's, the special accentuation of the "long measure" has been followed, and somewhat emphasized with a view to variety.

THE ODE OF LEBÍD.

GONE are they the lost camps, light flittings, long sojournings
in Miná, in Ghául̇a, Rijám left how desolate.
Lost are they. Rayyan lies lorn with its white torrent beds,
scored in lines like writings left by the flood-water.
Tent-floors smooth, forsaken, bare of all that dwelt in them,
years how long, the war-months, months too of peace-pleasures.
Spots made sweet with Spring-rains fresh-spilled from the Zodiac,
showers from clouds down-shaken, wind-wracks and thunder-clouds;
Clouds how wild of night-time, clouds of the dawn darkening,
clouds of the red sunset,—all speak the name of her.

Here, in green thorn-thickets, does bring forth how fearlessly;
here the ostrich-troops come, here too the antelopes.
Wild cows, with their wild calf-sucklings, standing over them,
while their weanlings wander wide in the bare valleys.
Clean-swept lie their hearth-stones, white as a new manuscript
writ with texts fresh-graven, penned by the cataracts,
Scored with lines and circles, limned with rings and blazonings,
as one paints a maid's cheek point-lined in indigo.
All amazed I stood there. How should I make questionings?
Dumb the rocks around me, silent the precipice,
Voices lost, where these dwelt who at dawn abandoning
tent and thorn-bush fencing fled to the wilderness.
Now thy sad heart acheth, grieveth loud remembering
girls how closely howdahed, awned with what canopies.
Every howdah curtained, lined with gauze embroideries,
figured with festoons hung red from the pole of it.
Trooped they there the maid-folk, wild white cows of Túdiha,
ay, or does of Wújra, long-necked, their fawns with them,
Fled as the mirâge flees, fills the vale of Bíshata,
fills the tree-clad wádies, íthel and rock-mazes.

What of her, Nowára, thy lost love, who fled from thee,
every heart-link sundered, close loop and free fetter!
Hers the Mórra camp-fires lit how far in Faïda,
in Hejáz what marches! How shalt thou win to her?
Eastward move they marching, to Muhájjer wandering
camped in Tái, in Férda, ay, in Rukhám of it.

Southward on to Yémen, to Sowéyk their sojournings,
to Waháf el Káhri, ay, and Tilkhám of it.
Man, have done! forget her,—one too far to comfort thee!
Who would his love garner first let him sunder it.
Shed the love that fails thee. Strong be thou, and break with her.
Keep thy gifts for friendship, freed from thy wilderment.
Mount thee on thy nága. Travel-trained and hard she is,
low her back with leanness, lessened the hump of her;
Shrunk her sides and wasted, jaded with long journeyings,
spare as her hide shoe-straps frayed by her road-faring.
Light she to her halter, to thy hand that guideth her,
as a red cloud southwards loosed from its rain-burden.
Nay a fair wild-ass she; at her side the white-flanked one,
he the scarred ass-stallion, bitten and struck for her.
Climbed they two the hill-top, he the bite-scarred ass-tyrant
her new mood resenting, being in foal to him.
On the crags high posted watcheth he from Thálabut
all the plain to guard her, ambushes laid for her.
Six months of Jumáda wandered have they waterless,
browsing the moist herbage, he her high sentinel.
Till returned their thirsting, need of the far water clefts,
all their will to win there speeding them waterwards.
What though with heels wounded, still the hot wind driveth them,
as a furnace burning, fire-scorched the breath of it.
In their trail a dust-cloud, like a smoke it wavereth,
like a fire new-lighted, kindling the flame of it,
Flame fanned by the North-wind, green wood mixed with dry fuel,
smoke aloft high curling. So is the dust of them.
He, when her pace slackened, pushed her still in front of him.
Nay, she might not falter, tyrant he urged her on,
Till they reached the streamlet, plunged and slaked their thirst in it,
A spring welling over, crest-high the reeds of it;
All its banks a cane-brake, thick with stems o'ershadowing;
bent are some, some standing, night-deep the shade of them.

Say is this her likeness? Or a wild cow wolf-raided
of her sweet calf loitering, she is the van of them.
She, the short-nosed, missed it. Lows she now unendingly,
roams the rocks, the sand-drifts, mourning and bellowing,
Lows in rage beholding that white shape, the limbs of it,
dragged by the grey wolf-cubs,—who shall their hunger stay?

Theirs the chance to seize it, hers the short forgetfulness.
  Death is no mean archer. Mark how his arrows hit.
Stopped she then at night-fall, while the rain in long furrows
  scored the bush-grown hill-slopes, ceaseless the drip of it,
Dripped on her dark back-line, poured abroad abundantly:
  not a star the heaven showed, cloud-hung the pall of it;
One tree all her shelter, standing broad-branched, separate
  at the sand-hills' edge-line, steep-set the sides of them.
She, the white cow, shone there through the dark night luminous,
  like a pearl of deep-seas, freed from the string of it.
Thus till morn, till day-dawn folded back night's canopy;
  then she fled bewildered, sliding the feet of her,
Fled through the rain lakelets, to the pool Suwáyada,
  all a seven nights' fasting twinned with the days of them,
Till despaired she wholly, till her udder milk-stricken
  shrank, so full to feed him suckling or weaning him.
Voices now she hears near, human tones, they startle her,
  though to her eye naught is: Man! he, the bane of her!
Seeketh a safe issue, the forenoon through listening,
  now in front, behind now, fearing her enemy.
And they failed, the archers. Loosed they then to deal with her
  fine-trained hounds, the lop-eared, slender the sides of them.
These outran her lightly. Turned she swift her horns on them,
  like twin spears of Sámhar, sharp-set the points of them.
Well she knew her danger, knew if her fence failed with them
  hers must be the red death. Hence her wrath's strategy.
And she slew Kasábi, foremost hound of all of them,
  stretched the brach in blood there, ay, and Sukhám of them.
Thus is she, my nága. When at noon the plains quiver
  and the hills dance sun-steeped, cloaked in the heat-tremors,
Ride I and my deeds do, nor forbear from wantoning,
  lest the fools should shame me, blame me the fault-finders.

Do not thou misprize me, thou Nowára. One am I
  binder of all love-knots, ay, and love's sunderer;
One who when love fails him, wails not long but flies from it;
  one whom one alone holds, hard death the hinderer.
What dost thou of mirth know, glorious nights, ah, how many—
  cold nor heat might mar them—spent in good company?
Came I thus discoursing to his sign, the wine-seller's
  drank at the flag-hoisting, drank till the wine grew dear,

Bidding up each full skin,—black with age the brand of it,
pouring forth the tarred jars, breaking the seals of them;
Pure deep draughts of morning, while she played, the sweet singer
fingering the lute-strings, showing her skill to me.
Ere the cock had crowed once, a first cup was quaffed by me:
ere slow man had stretched him, gone was the second cup.
On what dawns sharp-winded clothed have I the cold with it,
dawns that held the North-wind reined in the hands of them.
Well have I my tribe served, brought them aid and armament,
slept, my mare's reins round me, night-long their sentinel;
Ridden forth at day-dawn, climbed the high-heaped sand-ridges
hard by the foe's marches, dun-red the slopes of them;
Watched till the red sun dipped hand-like in obscurity,
till the night lay curtained, shrouding our weaknesses;
And I came down riding, my mare's neck held loftily
as a palm fruit-laden,—woe to the gatherer!
Swift was she, an ostrich; galloped she how wrathfully,
from her sides the sweat streamed, lightening the ribs of her;
Strained on her her saddle; dripped with wet the neck of her,
the white foam-flakes wreathing, edging the girth of her;
Thrusteth her neck forward, shaketh her reins galloping;
flieth as the doves fly bound for the water-springs.

At the King's Court strangers thronged from what far provinces,
each athirst for bounty, fearing indignity.
Stiff-necked they as lions in their hate, the pride of them,
came with stubborn proud feet, Jinns of the wilderness.
Stopped I their vain boastings, took no ill-tongued words from them,
let them not take licence. What were their chiefs to me?
I it was provided camels for their slaughtering,
I who their shares portioned, drawing the lots for them.
Every mouth I feasted. Barren mount and milch-camel
slew I for all daily. All shared the meat of them.
Far guest and near neighbour, every man rose satisfied,
full as in Tebála, fed as in green valleys.
Ay, the poor my tent filled, thin poor souls like sick-camels,
nágas at a tomb tied, bare-backed, no shirt on them.
Loud the winter winds howled; piled we high the meat-dishes;
flowed the streams of fatness, feeding the fatherless.
Thus the tribes were trysted; nor failed we the provident
to name one, a wise man, fair-tongued, as judge for them,

One who the spoil portioned, gave to each his just measure,
  spake to all unfearing, gave or refused to give,
A just judge, a tribe-sheykh, wise, fair-worded, bountiful,
  sweet of face to all men, feared by the warriors.

Noble we; our fathers wielded power bequeathed to them,
  dealt law to the nations, each tribe its lawgiver.
All our lineage faultless, no light words our promises;
  not for us the vain thoughts, passions of common men.
Thou fool foe, take warning, whatso the Lord portioneth
  hold it a gift granted, dealt thee in equity.
Loyalty our gift was, faith unstained our heritage;
  these fair things He gave us, He the distributor.
For for us a mansion built He, brave the height of it,
  lodged therein our old men, ay, and the youths of us,
All that bore our burdens, all in our tribe's sore sorrow,
  all that were our horsemen, all our high councillors.
Like the Spring are these men, joy to them that wait on them,
  to the weak, the widows, towers in adversity.
Thus our kin stands faith-firm, purged of tribe-malingerers.
  Woe be to all false friends! woe to the envious!

FIFTH ODE.

ÁNTARA.

OF all the pre-Islamic poets, 'Antara, or 'Antar, as he is more commonly called, has gained the widest celebrity, this less through the high merits of his verse, than for his exploits as a warrior and as the hero of the mediaeval romance which bears his name. He was indeed the true prototype of the Knights errant of our own Age of Chivalry, and, like Charlemagne and King Arthur, has a legendary character which it is somewhat difficult to separate from his character in history.

What is attributed to him as authentic by the Oriental learned is as follows: 'Antara was of the tribe of Abs, son of its supreme Sheykh Sheddád by an Abyssinian slave woman who gave him her dark countenance and with it the slur of illegitimacy still appertaining to such mixed offspring in Bedouin Arabia, and which the humaner law of Islám has been powerless there to efface. He was therefore despised and sent as a young man to herd his father's camels with the rest of the household slaves. Nevertheless he aspired to the love of his cousin, the nobly born 'Abla, and, according to the Arabian custom which recognizes in cousins a first right to the hand of every girl, asked her in marriage. The stain in his lineage, however, caused him to be refused, and it was only through the repeated necessity of the tribe in their long wars with Dobián that he at last overcame their prejudice. When the tents were in danger of pillage, Sheddád called on 'Antar to defend them, and 'Antar, whose valour alone could save the tribe from destruction and the women from captivity, claimed his reward as one who had been recognized by this summons as a son; and, though still, more than once, refused, eventually he was accorded his full right.

With the exception of this passion for 'Abla and his verses concerning her, 'Antar's life was an unbroken sequence of raids, battles, and reprisals, and as long as he lived there could be no peace with the enemy. He died, however, at last, slain in battle against the tribe of Táï, about the year 615; and it was then that, by the intervention of El Hárith, peace was finally made.

The romance of 'Antar, written in the second century of Islam, bears the traces of its spurious pre-Islamic character in the jinns and other supernatural beings who constantly are made to intervene in the affairs of its hero. Nevertheless it is interesting as a record of the age, early though not pre-Islamic, in which it was produced, and still more as being the most important of the Oriental originals on which some of our own Christian romances of the Middle Ages were founded. Its extreme length has hitherto prevented its being translated in full into English, but Mr. Terrick Hamilton published a sufficient selection of its chief incidents as long ago as 1819, saying of it in his preface that it was "now for the first time in part submitted to the European public." In the East, though popular with the multitude, and a favourite subject of recitation in the bazaars of Cairo and Damascus, it stands in small repute with scholars, who are intolerant of the vulgarisms which have crept into its text. It contains, however, much that would be found good poetry, if really well translated into English verse. Hamilton's rendering is wholly in prose, and prose of the Latinised conventional type, common in the England of his day:

"Abla's spirit appeared to me in my sleep. Thrice I kissed her within the veil.

It bade me adieu, but it deposited in me a flame that I feel burning through my bones.

Were I not left in solitude, and could I not quench the fire of my passion with tears, my heart would melt.

But I do not complain, though all my fears are on thy account, O thou perfect full moon.

O daughter of Málik, how can I be consoled, since my love for thee originated from the time I was weaned?

How can I hope to approach thee while the lions of the forest guard thy tent?

By the truth of my love for thee, my heart can never be cured but by patience.

O thou noble maid, till I exalt myself to the heights of glory with the thrusts of my spear and the blows of my sword, I will expose myself to every peril whenever the spears clash in the battle dust. Then shall I either be tossed upon the spear-heads, or be numbered among the noble."

Such is Hamilton's rendering of lines believed to be authentically 'Antara's, and which have been incorporated with others into the Romance. 'Antara's Moállaka, however, about which there is no doubt, is superior to any of these. It has all the best qualities of the pre-Islamic poetry and possesses a fire and energy, alternating with little touches of tenderness, perhaps superior to any of its rivals. It was written apparently at a time, after his first romance with 'Abla, when the stress of war and the long quarrel with her kinsmen had separated him from her. 'Antara records in it his early love, and how it had been crossed:

"O thou my lamb, the forbidden, prize of competitors!
Why did they bid me not love thee? Why wert thou veiled from me?"

Also his poem contains a description of his horse 'Abjer, which appeals more strongly to our modern love of animals, than anything, perhaps, that can be found in ancient poetry, where sympathy of that kind was very little understood. It has, too, the merit of being freer from the taint of politics, than any, except Imr-El-Káis'. 'Antara was no frequenter of the princely Courts either of Híra or Ghassán, and all his loves and hates were purely of the desert.

THE ODE OF ÁNTARA.

HOW many singers before me! Are there yet songs unsung?
Dost thou, my sad soul, remember where was her dwelling place?
Tents in Jiwá, the fair wádi, speak ye to me of her.
Fair house of 'Abla my true love, blessing and joy to thee!
Doubting I paused in the pastures, seeking her camel-tracks,
high on my swift-trotting nága tall as a citadel,
Weaving a dream of the past days, days when she dwelt in them,
'Abla, my true love, in Házzen, Sammán, Mutathéllemi.
There on the sand lay the hearth-stones, black in their emptiness,
desolate more for the loved ones fled with Om Héythami,
Fled to the land of the lions, roarers importunate.
Daily my quest of thee darkens, daughter of Mákhrami.

Truly at first sight I loved her, I who had slain her kin,
ay, by the life of thy father, not in inconstancy.
Love, thou hast taken possession. Deem it not otherwise.
Thou in my heart art the first one, first in nobility.
How shall I win to her people? Far in Anéyzateyn
feed they their flocks in the Spring-time, we in the Gháïlem.
Yet it was thou, my beloved, willed we should sunder thus,
bridled thyself the swift striders, black night encompassing.
Fear in my heart lay a captive, seeing their camel-herds
herded as waiting a burden, close to the tents of them,
Browsing on berries of khímkhim, forty-two milch-camels,
black as the underwing feathers set in the raven's wing.
Then was it 'Abla enslaved thee showing her tenderness,
white teeth with lips for the kissing. Sweet was the taste of them,
Sweet as the vials of odours sold by the musk sellers,
fragrant the white teeth she showed thee, fragrant the mouth of her.
So is a garden new planted fresh in its greenery,
watered by soft-falling raindrops, treadless, untenanted.
Lo, on it rain-clouds have lighted, soft showers, no hail in them,
leaving each furrow a lakelet bright as a silverling.
Pattering, plashing they fell there, rains at the sunsetting,
wide-spreading runlets of water, streams of fertility,
Mixed with the humming of bees' wings droning the daylight long,
never a pause in their chaunting, gay drinking-choruses.
Blithe iteration of bees' wings, wings struck in harmony,
sharply as steel on the flint-stone, light-handed smithy strokes.

Sweet, thou shalt rest till the morning all the night lightly there,
while I my red horse bestriding ride with the forayers.
Resting-place more than the saddle none have I, none than he
war-horse of might in the rib-bones—deep is the girth of him.

Say, shall a swift Shadaníeh bear me to her I love,
one under ban for the drinker, weaned of the foal of her,
One with the tail carried archwise, long though the march hath been,
one with the firm foot atrample, threading the labyrinths?
Lo, how she spurneth the sand-dunes, like to the ear-less one,
him with the feet set together; round him young ostriches
Troop like the cohorts of Yémen, herded by 'Ajemis,
she-camel cohorts of Yémen, herded by stammerers.
Watching a beacon they follow, led by the crown of him
carried aloft as a howdah, howdah where damsels sit,
Him the small-headed, returning, fur-furnished Ethiop,
black slave, to Thu-el-Ashíra;—there lie his eggs in it.
Lo, how my nága hath drunken deeply in Dóhradeyn;
how hath she shrunk back in Déylam, pools of the enemy,
Shrunk from its perilous cisterns, scared by the hunting one,
great-headed shrieker of evening, clutched to the flank of her.
Still to her off-side she shrinketh, deemeth the led-cat there
Clawing the more that she turneth;—thus is her fear of them.
Lo, she hath knelt in Ridá-a, pleased there and murmuring
soft as the sweet-fluting rushes crushed by the weight of her.
Thickly as pitch from the boiling oozeth the sweat of her,
pitch from the cauldron new-lighted, fire at the sides of it,
Oozeth in drops from the ear-roots. Wrathful and bold is she,
proud in her gait as a stallion hearing the battle-cry.

Though thou thy fair face concealest still in thy veil from me,
yet am I he that hath captured horse-riders how many!
Give me the praise of my fair deeds. Lady, thou knowest it,
kindly am I and forbearing, save when wrong presseth me.
Only when evil assaileth, deal I with bitterness;
then am I cruel in vengeance, bitter as colocynth.

Sometime in wine was my solace. Good wine, I drank of it,
suaging the heat of the evening, paying in white money,
Quaffing in goblets of saffron, pale-streaked with ivory,
hard at my hand their companion, the flask to the left of me.

Truly thus bibbing I squandered half my inheritance;
yet was my honour a wide word. No man had wounded it.
Since that when sober my dew-fall rained no less generous:
thou too, who knowest my nature, thou too be bountiful!
How many loved of the fair ones have I not buffeted,
youths overthrown! Ha, the blood-streams shrill from the veins of them.
Swift-stroke two-handed I smote him, thrust through the ribs of him;
forth flowed the stream of his life-blood red as anemone.
Ask of the horsemen of Málek, O thou his progeny,
all they have seen of my high deeds. Then shalt thou learn of them
How that I singly among them, clad in war's panoply,
stout on my war-horse the swift one charged at their chivalry.
Lo, how he rusheth, the fierce one, singly in midst of them,
waiting anon for the archers closing in front of us.
They that were nearest in battle, they be my proof to thee
how they have quailed at my war-cry, felt my urbanity.
Many and proud are their heroes, fear-striking warriors,
men who nor flee nor surrender, yielding not easily.
Yet hath my right arm o'erborne them, thrust them aside from me,
laid in their proud backs the long spear,—slender the shaft of it.
See, how it splitteth asunder mail-coat and armouring;
not the most valiant a refuge hath from the point of it.
Slain on the ground have I left him, prey to the lion's brood,
feast of the wrists and the fingers. Ha, for the sacrifice!

Heavy his mail-coat, its sutures, lo, I divided them
piercing the joints of the champion; brave was the badge of him.
Quick-handed he with the arrows, cast in the winter-time,
raider of wine-sellers' sign-boards, blamed as a prodigal.
He, when he saw me down riding, making my point at him,
showed me his white teeth in terror, nay, but not smilingly.
All the day long did we joust it. Then were his finger tips
stained as though dipped in the íthlem, dyed with the dragon's blood,
Till with a spear-thrust I pierced him, once and again with it,
last, with a blade of the Indies, fine steel its tempering,
Smote him, the hero of stature, tall as a tamarisk,
kinglike, in sandals of dun hide, noblest of all of them.

Oh, thou, my lamb, the forbidden! prize of competitors,
why did they bid me not love thee? why art thou veiled from me?
Sent I my hand-maiden spy-like: Go thou, I said to her,
bring me the news of my true love, news in veracity.

Go. And she went, and returning: These in unguardedness
  sit, and thy fair lamb among them, waiting thy archery.
Then was it turned she towards me, fawn-necked in gentleness,
  noble in bearing, gazelle-like, milk-white the lip of it.

Woe for the baseness of 'Amru, lord of ingratitude!
  Verily thanklessness turneth souls from humanity.
Close have I kept to the war-words thy father once spoke to me,
  how I should deal in the death-play, when lips part and teeth glitter,
When in the thick of the combat heroes unflinchingly
  cry in men's ears their defiance, danger forgot by them.
Close have I kept them and stood forth their shield from the enemy,
  calling on all with my war-cries, circling and challenging.
There where the horsemen rode strongest I rode out in front of them,
  hurled forth my war-shout and charged them;—no man thought blame of me.
Antar! they cried; and their lances, well-cords in slenderness,
  pressed to the breast of my war-horse still as I pressed on them.
Doggedly strove we and rode we. Ha, the brave stallion!
  now is his breast dyed with blood-drops, his star-front with fear of them!
Swerved he, as pierced by the spear-points. Then in his beautiful
  eyes stood the tears of appealing, words inarticulate.
If he had learned our man's language, then had he called to me:
  if he had known our tongue's secret, then had he cried to me.

Thus to my soul came consoling; grief passed away from it
  hearing the heroes applauding, shouting: Ho, Antar, ho!
Deep through the sand-drifts the horsemen charged with teeth grimly set,
  urging their war-steeds, the strong-limbed, weight bearers all of them.
Swift the delúls too I urged them, spurred by my eagerness
  forward to high deeds of daring, deeds of audacity.
Only I feared lest untimely drear death should shorten me
  e'er on the dark sons of Démdem vengeance was filled for me.
These are the men that reviled me, struck though I struck them not,
  vowed me to bloodshed and evil or e'er I troubled them.
Nay, let their hatred o'erbear me! I care not. The sire of them
  slain lies for wild beasts and vultures. Ha! for the sacrifice!

SIXTH ODE.

IBN KOLTHÚM.

AMR IBN KOLTHÚM, supreme Sheykh of the Béni Tághleb, stands in the first rank of pre-Islamic poets. He was born, it is said, before the beginning of the sixth century, was Sheykh of his tribe at the age of fifteen, and died at the century's close, twenty-two years before the Héjra.

It is related of his mother Léyla, daughter of Muhálhil, a woman who attained to a position of great honour afterwards among the Arabs, that, as was then a common custom, her father ordered her at her birth to be destroyed. But, having been warned in a dream, he spared her, and she grew up to be the mother of Amr.

Amr was hot-headed, proud and generous, popular with his tribesmen, and from his birth a poet. The occasion of his Ode, as related in the Kitáb-el-Agháni, and with variations by other commentators, was as follows:

The tribes of Tághleb and Bekr, who owned a common descent from their ancestor Wáïl, one of the primitive patriarchs of Arabian genealogy, had been long at war, on account of the slaying of Koléyb Ibn Robía, when Amr Ibn Hind, King of Híra, intervened to make peace between them. A condition imposed by the King was, that if any man should be found slain among them, that tribe in whose *díra*, or pastoral district, the body lay, should be held responsible for the blood-wite, and that if it lay in a neutral zone, the distance should be measured to the tents of the tribe nearest, and that tribe should be responsible. Also he took one hundred young men from either clan as hostages for the peace, and these rode always with the King, wherever he journeyed, whether for peace or war. Now it happened that in a march against the Béni Táï, the young men of Tághleb thus held as hostages perished by misadventure in the desert, of thirst, some say, and others of a poisonous wind, *simúm*. But the tribesmen of Tághleb affirmed that the cause of death was that they had been refused water at the wells of Tárfa, by the men of Sheybán, a section of the Béni Bekr, and they demanded of these the blood-wite. But the men of Bekr protested, saying: "It is you that would make trouble and rend the veil. The young men were on the road, and we gave them water, and they went their way. How should it be on us, if they went straying, and were lost in the wilderness?" And they appealed to Ibn Hind. And the men of Tághleb chose Amr Ibn Kolthúm, their Prince, to plead their cause at Híra; and the men of Bekr chose El Naamán. And both stood before the King. And Amr, as complainer in the case, was called upon first to speak. And he recited the verses which are his Ode of the Moállakát.

And it is related that when Amr had ended his pleading a dispute arose between him and El Náamán in presence of the King. And the King was angry with both, and he would not hear El Náamán, but called upon El Hárith Ibn Híliza, an ancient poet of the Bekr, to plead for Bekr in the place of Náamán. And El Hárith without more preparation recited his Ode in reply to Amr Ibn Kolthúm. Thus the two Odes are always quoted together, and there is no reason to doubt the truth of the story about them.

And it is said that when El Hárith was brought before Ibn Hind, it was perceived that he had a leprosy, so that the King sat behind the curtain of his tent to hear him. And in his eloquence, El Hárith, who stood leaning on his bow, did not take notice that his hand became cut by the bow-string. And Ibn Hind as he listened, bent forward more and more in admiration at his verses, and he bade him come within the curtain, and seated him at last beside him. And he gave his award to the Béni Bekr.

And it is also said that the award thus given was the cause of the King's death. For Amr Ibn Kolthúm, going away with the Tághleb, afterwards sought an occasion and slew the King. But others say that the reason was a vengeance for the death of his cousin, the poet Tárafa. And yet another account of the King's death is this: As Amr Ibn Hind was drinking one day with his companions at Híra, he asked of them, boasting, if they knew any man of the Arabs whose mother would be too proud to wait upon his own mother Hind. And it was told him that the mother of Amr Ibn Kolthúm would be too proud. And he asked them "Why?" And they said: "Her father was Muhálhil Ibn Robía, and her uncle Koléyb Ibn Waïl, the noblest men of the Arabs, and her husband is Kolthúm Ibn Málek, the best horseman of the Arabs, and her son is Amr, Lord of his people." And Ibn Hind sent messengers to Arabia to invite Amr Ibn Kolthúm to visit him at Híra and to bring with him his mother Leyla, to visit Hind. And he built a tent for them of skins, between Híra and the Euphrates, and he received them there. And when Léyla was alone with Hind in the tent, their two sons waiting without, and the dishes were brought them, that they might eat, then Hind said to Léyla: "Reach me, I pray you, of that dish." But Léyla answered quickly: "Let each who wants it serve herself to food." And Hind bade her again to bring it her. Then Léyla lifted up her voice and cried aloud: "O humilitation! To my help, ye Tághleb!" And her son heard her, and the blood rushed to his head. And Amr Ibn Hind was afraid, seeing evil in his guest's eyes. And Amr Ibn Kolthúm seized Amr Ibn Hind's sword where it hung in the tent—and it was the only sword there—and struck Ibn Hind with it on the head and he shouted to the Beni Tághleb. And they all drew their swords and plundered the camp, and drove away the running camels, and fled back to Arabia. And Amr made verses on what had happened, and the Beni Tághleb recited it in season and out of season, small and great, until they wearied the Arabs, and the song became as it were a by-word of repetition among them.

Such is the received account. The metre of the two Odes, Ibn Kolthúm's and El Hárith's, is shorter than that of the preceding five, but is not less brilliant. It is, perhaps, better adapted to the argumentative character of the poems and has a certain swing and resonance which is most attractive. The matter of them, being as it is mainly political, appeals indeed less strongly to the modern English reader. But to those well acquainted with contemporary Arabia they possess an extreme interest, as proving how little the Bedouin world has changed either in its political ideas or even its political position during the last fourteen hundred years. There is hardly an idea expressed by either of the pleaders that might not to-day be heard in the mouths of rival tribe-sheykhs who have journeyed to Háïl to lay their disputes before Ibn Rashíd. The only difference at the present day would be that the rival declamations would no longer be in verse.

ODE OF IBN KOLTHÚM.

HA! The bowl! Fill it high, a fair morning wine-cup!
  Leave we naught of the lees of Andarína.
Rise, pour forth, be it mixed, let it foam like saffron!
  tempered thus will we drink it, ay, free-handed.
Him who grieves shall it cure, his despites forgotten;
  nay, but taste it in tears, it shall console thee.
He, the hoarder of wealth, with the hard face fear-lined,
  whilst he tasteth, behold him freely giving.
Thou, O mother of Amru, the cup deniest;
  yet, the right is the wine should pass thy right-hand.
Not the worst of thy three friends is he thou scornest,
  he for whom thou hast poured no draught of morning.
O the cups that I quaffed in Baálabékki!
  O the bowls of Damascus, Kaisarína!
Sad fate stands at the door, and uninvited
  takes us marked for his own at the hour predestined.

Hold, draw rein, ere we sunder, sweet camel-rider;
  list awhile to my words, nor idly answer.
Wait. Of thee would I know how came the estrangement,
  whence this haste to betray a friend too faithful?
Tell the fear of that day, what blows! what woundings!
  what refreshment I poured on thy kin's eyelids!
Each to-day is foredoomed. And who knows to-morrow,
  who the after of days, the years we see not?

She her beauty shall show thee, if thou shouldst find her
  far from injurious eyes, in desert places.
Fair white arms shall she show, as a white she-camel's,
  pure as her's the long-necked one, yet unmounted.
Twin breasts smooth, shalt thou see, as of ivory polished,
  guarded close from the eyes, the hands of lovers.
Waist how supple, how slim! Thou shalt span it sweetly;
  fair flanks sloped to thine eyes and downward bending.
Broad her hips for desire, than thy tent door wider;
  nay, but thine is her waist, thine own for madness.
Ankles twain, as of marble, are hers. I hear them
  clanking, clattering on, as her anklets rattle.
None hath grieved as I grieve, not she, Om Sákbin,
  roaring loud for her lost one, her colt-camel.

None hath grieved as I grieve, not she, the mother
  mourning nine of her sons, her home their red grave.
So recalled I youth's time, and aloud with longing
  wept at thought of her gone, her howdah fleeting,
Till before me the plain of Yemâma spreading
  flashed, its points in the sun like a foe unsheathing.

O thou Lord Ibn Hind, be thy wrath less quick-breathed;
  wait the word of our mouth, the whole truth spoken,
How each day we ride forth, our banners pure-white,
  how each night we return, our banners red-dyed.
Days of fighting had we, and of joyous glory,
  whilst we smote at the king, his dues denying,
Whilst we vanquished the man their tribes had named king,
  him, the chief they had crowned, their world's-protector.
Stood our horses before him asweat with combat,
  wreathed the reins on their necks, their hind-feet resting.
Near him built we our tents, Dhu-tulúh our outpost,
  El Shamáat at our hand, his riders routed.
Fled the dogs of their tribes from our spear-points howling;
  lo, their thorn we have cut from root to branches.
They who came to our wheat-mill have known our mill-stones;
  they who came for our corn have been stayed for grinding.
Let the mill-cloth be spread in the East lands Nejd-wards;
  be our corn the Kodáat, their tribes assembled.
You as guests to our door in your guile came smiling;
  see, the high feast is served, yourselves the banquet.
Fairly entertained we and plied with victual;
  just at dawn it began, our mill-stone grinding.
We the tribes have supplied, have up-held their charges,
  borne the burden alone they laid upon us.
Pierced have we with our spear-points their backs the fleers,
  smitten low with our swords and pruned their proud ones.
Lances black of the Khótti are ours, how slender,
  swords that hiss in our hands, to impale and pare them.
Yea, the heads of their mighty have rolled before us,
  loads let loose on a road from beasts unburdened.
Still with might we assailed, we pushed, we pressed them,
  lopped their heads at the neck, laid bare their shoulders.
Hate for hate have we given, in deeds revealing
  all the strength of our wrong, our long-pent anger.

Heirs are we of our wrath, as Maád well knoweth;
glory deal we and wounds, as our right proveth.
When surprise is our lot and the tent-roofs tumble,
—sudden raid of the foe—we defend our neighbours.
Bite we sharp with our swords, nor apportion mercy,
swift ere these shall have seen the hand that smites them.
Reckless we in the melée, our swords with their swords;
wooden swords you had deemed theirs in hands of children;
Deemed our garments and theirs, their robes and our robes,
dyed had been in the vats—so red a purple!
Men there were in their fear held back and faltered;
terror clutched at their lips, their fate before them.
We alone, like Mount Ráhwa unmoved, in squadrons
stood protecting the weak, their battle-winners.
All we held in our youth to be slain for glory,
ay, and our gray-beard fighters, our old campaigners,
Doughty challengers we of them, all ill-comers,
Girt for crossing of swords, their sons with our sons,
This day going in fear of our children's fair lives,
faring forth in a band and as swift dispersing;
That day freed and secure, the alarm forgotten,
raiding we in our turn on a far-off foray.
Ours the Captain of Júshm, our chief Ibn Béker,
Breaker he of the tribes, of the weak, the strong tribes.
Not again shall they tell it, the envious nations,
how we humbled our heads awhile before them.
Not again shall they fool us or jest against us;
lo, the cheek of the proud with pride we out-cheek.

Tell us, Prince Ibn Hind, on what guile thou buildest?
how should we to thy kingship yield obedience?
Tell us, 'Amru the King, by what subtle reason
dreamest thou to cajole our slandered homage?
Words—nay, threats—thou hast hurled. But O 'Amru, softly!
these were well for thy slaves, thy mother's bondsmen.
Think! Our lances, how oft have other foemen
failed, before thee, to bend them, to make them pliant.
So the lance-head of iron which bites the lance-shaft,
twists to grip of the hand and makes a weapon;
Stiff it grows in the grasp, till aloft it jangles,
rives the head of the foe and his who forged it.

Who has dared thee to tell of Júshm Ibn Béker,
  him as wanting in war, our proud forefather?
Are not we too of 'Alkama, heirs in glory,
  his, the fortress of fame? To-day we hold it.
Come not we of Muhálhil? Nay, more and better,
  come not we of Zohéyr, of the nobles noblest.
Ours Attáb and Kolthúm, in ascent our fathers;
  we the heirs of their fame, our first possession.
We with Búrati too, as all wot, claim kinship,
  him, the shield of the weak, as we too shield them.
All are ours, and Koléyb the renowned great fighter.
  Whatso is in the world of fame is our fame.
Who dares link our she-camel with his, lo, straightway
  broken lieth the neck-rope, the neck too broken.
Firm are we in our faith. Thou shalt find none surer,
  no such men of their word to bind and loosen.
We, the day of the beacons on high Khazára,
  gave, and more, of our aid than all the aiders.
We the strong-hold of Thú-urát held how stoutly,
  starved our nagas within it on what lean pasture!
We the right wing defended, the day of battle;
  next us fought too the left wing, no less our brethren.
Whoso stood in their path have beheld them charging;
  whoso paused on our way we slew before us.
These returned with the plunder, with wealth made captive,
  we with lords in our train and kings in fetters.
Ho, ye children of Béker, aroint ye, boasters!
  Know ye nought of our name? Must ye learn our glory?
Nay, ye know of our valour, our hands with your hands,
  fights how fierce with the spears, with the arrows singing.
Helmets ours are of steel, stout shields from Yémen,
  tall the swords in our hands and poised for striking.
Mail-coats ours; in the sun you have seen them gleaming;
  hawberks wide for our swords, of a noble wideness.
Ay, and after the fight, you have seen us naked,
  creased the skin of our limbs like leathern jerkins,
Seen the bend of our backs, where the armour pressed us,
  scored with waves, like a pool the South-wind blowing.

Lo, the mares we bestride at the dawn of battle!
  sleek-coat mares, the choice ones; ourselves have weaned them.
Charge they mail-clad together, how red with battle,
  red the knots of their reins as dyed with blood-stains.

Are not these the inheritance of our fathers?
  shall not we to our sons in turn bequeath them?
We the vanguard in arms? Behind us marching
  trail our beautiful ones, our wives close-guarded.
They it was who imposed on our lives a promise,
  still their badge to uphold from all assaulting,
Ay, and plunder to bring, fair mares and helmets,
  noble prisoners, bound with ropes, to serve them.
Thus go we to the war. And behold, the clansmen
  seized with fear of us fly and form alliance,
While our maidens advance with a proud gait swaying,
  like to drinkers of wine, with spoils o'erladen,
Camel-riders each one, of Júshm Ibn Béker,
  beauty theirs and the blood, and all noble virtues,
Feeders sure of our mares. Yet they tell us lightly:
  none will we for our lovers, save the valiant.
Since the fence of the fair is but this, the sword-stroke,
  this, the shredding of limbs as a plaything shredded.
Thus say they, and we hear them, our swords unsheathing
  yet are all men our sons who kneel before us.
Heads we toss of the proud, as you see a ball tossed,
  kicked in play by the youths that urge the football.
All men know us of old in Maád, the tribesmen,
  when our tents we have built in the open pastures,
Feasters are we of men with the men that love us,
  slayers are we of men, the men that hate us;
Rightful lords of the plain, to forgive and welcome;
  where we will we have pitched. Who has dared gainsay us?
Still with ire we deny in the face of anger;
  still with smiles we accede to smiles of pleading.
Faithful aye to the weak who have made submission;
  ruthless aye to the proud who raise rebellion.
Ours the right of the wells, of the springs untroubled;
  theirs the dregs of the plain, the rain-pools trampled.
Nay, but ask of the tribes, of Tommáh, Domíyan,
  what the worth of our hands, of our hearts in battle.
Nay, but ask of the King, when he came to bend us,
  what of pride we returned to his words of evil.
Lo, the lands we o'errun, till the plains grow narrow,
  lo, the seas will we sack with our war-galleys.
Not a weanling of ours but shall win to manhood,
  find the world at his knees, its great ones kneeling.

SEVENTH ODE.

EL HÁRITH.

OF El Hárith Ibn Hílliza of the Béni Bekr, little is told us by the commentators except what has been already related, of his pleading the cause of his tribe, before Amr Ibn Hind, against that of Tághleb. Like all the rest of the Moállakát poets, he was of noble birth and a warrior. He was also long-lived, for it is said of him that he was already a hundred years old when he made his Golden Ode. If this can be taken as exact, it would make him by many years the earliest in point of birth of all these poets, for the pleading referred to took place about the year 560 A.D. Beyond the facts, however, connected with his Ode nothing definite is recorded of him.

His Ode is from first to last a piece of special pleading on a political subject, and for this reason will be found the least generally interesting of the seven. It is almost unadorned with those wild natural descriptions of beast and bird and tree, which make the chief charm of the others, nor is there much of originality or passion in its opening love-verses. These are introduced clearly as a matter of convention, and were in all probability borrowed in old age for the occasion from the poetry of his younger time. They have nothing in common with the rest of the Ode, and there is no echo of them in the body of the piece. The whole poem is a long argument vigorously expressed and not without a beauty of its own, but with more of flattery towards the prince addressed than was common among the pre-Islamic poets. Hind herself, the prince's mother, is said to have been pleased at the introduction of her name in the opening verses, and to have influenced Amr in El Hárith's favour. With regard to this, the commentator El Tabrízi gives some interesting details.

El Hárith, he relates, had prepared his Ode for the occasion, but he was bashful about reciting it, because of the leprosy with which he was afflicted, "For," said he when urged by his companions, "the King would bid me speak from behind seven curtains, and afterwards have my footsteps washed with water because of my malady." But in the end he was persuaded, and El Hárith recited his ode from behind the screen. Now Hind was listening, and when she heard his verses she exclaimed: "Talláhi! never saw I the like of this day, that such a man should speak from behind seven curtains!" And the King said "Remove a curtain," and they removed a curtain. And El Hárith advancing still recited. And they removed a second and a third curtain, and so all the seven, until he stood unhidden before the King. And the King bade him eat out of his own dish, and when he was gone gave order that no water should be sprinkled on his footsteps.

Thus El Hárith's pleading effected its purpose with Ibn Hind, and secured a verdict from him in favour of the singer's tribesmen. The Ode is full of allusions to somewhat obscure events, and the precise meaning of each verse is consequently difficult to give, but their explanation will be found, as far as it can be ascertained, in the notes at the end of this volume.

The metre is one known as *el khafíf* or the "light measure," and is here carefully reproduced. Moreover, owing to the accident that the first four couplets contain a string of proper names, it has been found possible to give in them a fair notion of the rhyme as well as the rhythm of the original, and the opening lines may therefore be taken as closer in sound to the Arabic than any others here translated.

THE ODE OF EL HÁRITH

LIGHTLY took she her leave of me, Asmá-u,
  went no whit as a guest who outstays a welcome;
Went forgetting our trysts, Burkát Shemmá-u,
  all the joys of our love, our love's home, Khalsá-u.
Muhayyátu, she thee forgets, Sifáhu,
  thee, Fitákon, Aádibon, thee Wafá-u.
Thee, Riád el Katá, thee, vale of Shérbub,
  'Anak, thee, Shobatána, and thee, Ablá-u.
Nay, ye lost are to me with my lost glory;
  nay, though tears be my meat, weeping wins no woman.
Yet, a snare to my eyes, afar was kindled
  fire by night on the hill. It was Hind's love-beacon.
Blindly now do I watch her from Khezáza;
  woe, the warmth of it, woe,—though the hilltops redden!
Woe its blaze from Akík, its flame from Shákhseyn!
  woe the signal alight for me, Hind's love-incense!

Out on tears and despair! I go free, sundered;
  here stand doors of relief. Who hath fled escapeth.
Mount I light on my nága. No hen ostrich
  swift as she, the tall trotter, her brood behind her,
Hearing voices who fled from them, the hunters,
  pressing fast on her way from mid-eve to nightfall.
Nay, behold her, my noble one, upheaving
  motes and dust on her path, as a cloud pursuing.
All un-shooed are the feet of her, her sandals
  strewn how wide on her road by the rough rocks loosened.
Joy thus take I on her, the summer heat through.
  All but I had despaired,—like a blinded camel.

O the curse of men's eyes, of their ill-speaking!
  Danger deep and a wound did their false lips deal us.
Have not these with their tongues made small things great things,
  telling lies of our lives, our kind kin, the Arákim?
Mixing blame with un-blame for us, till flouted
  stand we, proven of wrong, with the guilty guiltless.

All, say these, that have run with us the wild ass,
ours are they, our allies, as our own tribe their tribes.
Thus by night did they argue it and plot it,
rose at dawn to their treason and stood forth shouting.
Loud the noise of their wrath. This called, that answered;
great the neighings of steeds and the camel roarings.

Ho, thou weaver of wild words, thou tale-painter!
must it thus be for ever and thus with Amru?
Not that slanders are strange. Their words we heed not;
long ere this have we known them, their lips, the liars.
High above them we live. Hate may not harm us,
fenced in towers of renown, our unstained bright honour.
Long hath anger assailed us, rage, denial;
long hath evil prevailed in the eyes of evil.
Nathless, let them assault. As well may Fortune
hurl its spears at the rocks, at the cloud-robed mountains.
Frowneth wide of it Fear. Fate shall not shake it.
Time's worst hand of distress shall disturb it never.

O thou king Iramíyan! with thee circle
riders keen of their steel to cut off thy foemen.
King art thou, the all-just, of Earth's high walkers
foremost, first in the World, its all-praise surpassing.
If of wrong there be aught untamed, unstraightened,
bring but word to our chiefs; they shall deal out justice.
Set thy gaze on the hills, on Mílha, Sákib.
See the slain unavenged, while alive their slayers.
Probe the wounds of our anger, though thou hurt us,
yet shall truth be approved and the falsehood flouted.
Else be thou of us silent, and we silent,
closing lids on our wrong, though the mote lies under.
Yet, refusing the peace, whomso you question,
he shall speak in our praise, shall assign us worship.

O the days of the war, of our free fighting,
radings made in surprise, the retreats, the shoutings!
How our nágas we scourged from Sâf el Bahreyn,
pressing hard to the end, to our goal El Hása!
Turned had we on Temím before Mohárrem,
taken their daughters for wives, their maids for handmaids.

None might stay us nor strive with us. The stoutest
turned, though turning availed not nor their feet flying,
Nay, nor mountain might hide nor plain protect them;
blackness burnt in the sun, it might bring no succour.
Thou, O King, art the master. Where in all lands
standeth one of thy height? There is none beside thee.

Lo, how stiff was our stand for him, El Móndir.
Say, were we, as were these, Ibn Hind's base herdsmen?
Let the Tághlebi slain in their blood answer,
unavenged where they lie. In the dust we spilled it.
He, the king, when in that high place Maisúna's
tent he builded, for her who so loved Ausá-u,
What of turbulent folk did he there gather,
broken men of the tribes, ragged, hungry vultures!
Dates and water to all he gave in bounty.
God's revenge on the guilty they called his soldiers.
You the weight of them proved with your mad challenge,
brought them blind on your back by your idle boasting.
Nay, they gave you no false words, laid no ambush;
broad before you at noon you beheld them marching.

Ho, thou bearer of tales to Amru, babbler!
when of this shall the end be, how soon the silence?
Proofs he hath at our hands, three honest tokens,
each enough for his eyes of our faith unswerving.
First when came from Shakík at him the war-lords,
all Maád in their tribes, with each clan a banner.
Mail-clad men were there there, their chieftain Káis,
he, the Prince Karathíyan, a rock, a stronghold.
With him sons of the brave, of freeborn ladies;
naught might stand to their shock save alone our sword-blades.
Them we drove back with wounds like the out-rushing
streams when goat-skins are pricked; it was thus their blood flowed;
Drove them back to Thahlána its strong places,
scattered, drenched in their gore where the thigh wounds spouted.
Struck we stern at the lives of them; then trembled
deep our spears in their well, like a long-roped bucket.
Only God shall appraise how we misused them;
none hath claimed for their lives the uncounted blood price.
Next with Hójra it was, Ibn om Katáma;
with him rode the Iráni,—how red their armour!

Roused, a lion, he chargeth, his feet thudding,
  yet as Spring to the poor in their day of hunger.
Chains we struck from the hands of Imr el Káis;
  long the days of his grief were, his months of bondage.
We, when Jaun of Aâl Beni 'Aus sought us,
  rock-strong with him a band of unyielding horsemen,
Nothing feared, though the dust of them around us
  swept the plain like a smoke by the war-flame kindled.
Put we swords on his neck, Ghassán, for Móndir,
  wrath that less than our right was the blood price counted.
Lastly brought we the nine of the blood royal,
  all their wealth in our hands, an unnumbered booty.
Amr a son was of ours Ibn Om Eyyási;
  close in kinship he came, when he gave the dowry.
Let this stand to our count, our power in pleading!
  land with land are we knit, by the strong ones strengthened.
Hold the tongue of your boasting, your vain glory,
  else be yourselves the blind, on yourselves ill-fortune.

O, remember the oath of Thil Majázi,
  all that was of old time, the fair words, the pledges.
Flee the evil, the hate! Shall men gainsay it,
  that which stands on the skin, for the whim of any?
Think how we with yourselves the fair deed signed there,
  did the thing we should do, and no less, our duty.
Faction all and injustice! As well, when feasting,
  take, for vow of a sheep, a gazelle in payment!
Was it ours, say, the blame of it all, when Kíndah
  took your booths for a spoil, that of us you claim it?
Was it ours that foul deed of him, Eyádi?
  are we bound with his rope, like a loaded camel?
Not by us were these done to their death, nor Káis,
  nay, nor Jéndal by us, nor he Haddá-u.
Theirs, not ours, were the crimes of Beni Atíkeh;
  clean of blame are our hands since you tore the treaties.
Eighty went of Temím,—in their right hands lances;
  each a sentence of death, when they went against you,
Left your sons where they lay sword-slashed and blood-stained,
  brought a tumult of spoil till men's ears were deafened.
Is it ours the ill-deed of the man Hanífa?
  ours the strife of all time, Earth's arrears of evil?

EL HÁRITH

Ours the wrong of Kodáat? Nay, 'tis all injustice;
not for these and their sins are our hands indicted.
Not for these, nor their raid on the Béni Rázah;
who shall approve their claim in Nitá, in Búrka?
Long they cringed for a spoil, these camel-cravers,
yet not one did we give, not a black nor white one;
Left them bare till they fled with their backs broken,
all unwatered their thirst, unassuaged their vengeance;
Horsemen hard on their track, El Fellak's riders,
pity none in their hand, in their heart no sparing.
Ours it was, the dominion of all these peoples,
ours till El Móndir ruled, the sweet rain of heaven.

Thou, O King, art the master. Thou our witness
stoodst the day of Hayáreyn. Our proof is proven!

NOTE ON THE INTRODUCTION.

A PORTION of this Introduction appeared some years ago, together with extracts from the verses and the greater part of the Ode of 'Antara, under the title of "The Poetry of the Arabian Ignorance," in the pages of the "New Review." These are here reproduced with permission from the representatives of the copyright.

The system of transliteration followed in the rendering of the Arabic names throughout the volume is that usually adopted by geographers and historians, no attempt being made by means of dots or symbols to distinguish accurately between the various forms of the Arabic consonants. Such symbols, useful as they are in works of erudition, would, the translators think, only confuse the general reader, for whose assistance simple accents have been placed on the syllables of each word where the stress in speaking naturally falls.

In like manner no attempt has been made to deal with the intricacies of Arabic prosody as expounded by the Grammarians ancient and modern. These are of such extreme complexity that compared with them the rules of Greek verse-writing would seem to be mere child's play, and they are absolutely incapable of being applied to any other language than that out of which they sprang. They are indeed an example of pedantry gone mad, and their evolution in the schools of Kufa during the two first centuries of Islam is almost enough by itself to explain the decay there of the national poetry. To translators they can only prove a stumbling-block and are best ignored. English students, however, who are curious in these matters may find all that is known to European scholarship on the subject in Professor Palmer's "Arabic Grammar" (1874), where the prosody of the language is exhaustively treated.

NOTES ON ÍMR EL KÁIS.

'Imr-el-Káis ibn Héjr. Some of the early commentators have thrown doubt on this being the poet's true name, which is given by Ibn Kásim el Mághrabi as Jéndah, with the explanation that 'Imr-el-Káis was a pseudonym only. 'Imr-el-Káis, these say, signifies "The man of Grief"; and the nickname was applied to the poet on account of his misfortunes. Sheykh Mohámmed 'Abdu, however, who is our greatest living Arabic scholar, holds this to be altogether a mistake. The meaning of 'Imr-el-Káis, he affirms, is simply the "man," in the sense of the "slave," of Káis, Káis being one of the gods of the pagan Arabs, and the name was used constantly as a proper name by them, just as now 'Abd-Alláh, Slave of God, is used by the Moslems, and 'Abd-el-Messíh, slave of the Messiah, by the Christians. It is true that Káis has a meaning of grief or trouble, and it is probable that the idol so named was a tutelary deity of consolation. The Greek chroniclers, it may be remarked, speak of the poet simply as Káis.

Kings of Kíndi. The Kings of Kíndi were members of the ancient royal race of Hímyar, and ruled a portion of Yémen under the supreme Head of their family, the Tóbba, by which name or title the Yemenite Emperors were known. 'Abu Obeyda, a historian of the time of the Caliph Harún El Rashíd, relates that the manner in which they acquired their kingship was that in the days of the Hímyarite monarchy, certain tribes descended from

Wáil, finding themselves in a condition of disorder through the lack of a supreme Chief, held council, and they said: "The fools among us have gotten the upper hand and the strong among us eat up the weak. Let us go to the Tóbba, that he may place a ruler over us." And the Tóbba placed them under his kinsman Héjr 'Akil-el-Marár of Kíndi, and Héjr and his sons after him ruled over them. And Héjr the father of 'Imr-el-Káis was great-grandson of that first Héjr. And the same thing happened also to him, for the tribes of 'Asad and Ghatafán chose him for a like reason to be their ruler. The Kings of Kíndi were the last of the Hímyarites to hold rule in Yémen, being driven back to the original home of Hímyar in Hádramaut in the last century before Islám.

Saalík. The "broken men" of the tribes who, for various offences against tribal morality, had been expelled from or had forsaken the community of their fellows. Such fugitives still to the present day form bands of outlawed robbers, and are far more dangerous for the wayfarer than are the members of an ordinary Bedouin raid. They live in the mountains, inhabiting rocks and caves, wherever such are to be found in Arabia. Under the name of *habalís* they are thus described by Mr. Doughty in his "Arabia Deserta": "The *habalís,*" he says, "desert fiends, are dreaded by the nomad tribesmen, as the Beduw themselves among settled country and oasis folk. Commonly the *habalís* are some young miscreants that having hardly any head of cattle at home, will desperately cast themselves upon every cruel hazard: yet others are strenuous, solitary men, whose unquiet mettle moves them from slothing in the tent's shadow to prowl as the wolf in the wilderness. These outlaws, enduring intolerable hardships, are often of an heathenish cruelty; it is pretended they willingly leave none alive. Nearly always footmen, they are more hardly perceived, lurking under crag and bush."

His first wife. It is not known who the first wife of 'Imr-el-Káis was, except that she was a girl of good family. She was travelling with her father, in the night time, when 'Imr-el-Káis overtook them and rode on with them. And it is related in the Kitáb el Agháni that when he had asked her, "O, maiden, what are the 8 and the 4 and the 2?" and when she had answered him as stated in the text, and he had demanded her of her father in marriage, she arranged with him that on the day when he should come to take her she should put to him in her turn three questions, so that she might recognize that it was indeed he and no other. And when the time came for him to claim her, 'Imr el-Káis sent on before him his servant with a goat-skin of butter and a goat-skin of honey and a suit of fine dyed garments. But the servant on his way stopped at a well for water, and, having unfolded the suit, through vanity put it on, and he opened also the skins and feasted those whom he found at the watering, but afterwards when he would put off the garments they caught in his hair and were torn. And in this plight he passed on to the girl's tribe, and the fighting men were away. And he inquired of her as to her father and her mother and her brethren, and he gave her the gifts. And she said to him, "Return and tell thy lord that my father hath gone to bring near that which was far, and to make far that which was near; and that my mother hath gone to make of one soul two souls, and that my brother is at watch for the setting of the sun, and that your heaven is rent asunder and that your two storehouses have overflowed." And the young man returned to his lord and gave him the message. And 'Imr-el-Káis understood its meaning, and knew that her father had gone to make alliances with the tribes, and that her mother was with a neighbour attending a birth, and that her brother was with his flocks waiting for the night that he might travel on with them, and that the garments he had sent had been worn by his servant and rent, and that the goat-skins had been opened. And the man confessed and said, "I was at the watering-place of the Arabs and they asked me as to my birth, and I said that I was my lord's cousin, and I put on your robe and it was torn, and I opened the skins and feasted the people." And 'Imr-el-Káis said, "*'Awlalak!* woe to thee!" And he drove the camels he had promised to his bride before him, and with them that servant. And when they alighted the servant went to water the camels and 'Imr-el-Káis to help him. And while he was helping him the servant pushed him into the well; and he went on alone to the girl's tribe. And the man told the women that he was the bridegroom come for the girl. And the news was brought to her, "Thy bridegroom is here for thee." And the girl answered, "I know not whether he be my bridegroom or no, but slay for him a camel and give him to eat, and let it be of the paunch and the tail." And they did so, and he ate. And she said, "Give him to drink, but let it be of the sour milk." And he drank of it. And she said, "Spread for him the carpet, but let it be near to the offal and the blood." And the servant lay down and slept. And when the girl arose in the morning she sent to the young man and said, "I would put questions to thee." And he answered, "As thou wilt." And she asked, "For what shall thy two lips be moved?" And he said, "For kissing thee." And she asked, "And for what shalt thou stir thy two sides?" And he said, "The need to embrace thee." And she asked again, "And thy thighs, what shall stir them?" And he answered, "The desire to come to thee." And she said, "He is a slave. Bind his hands." And they did so.

But, while this was doing, some men who were passing by drew 'Imr-el-Káis from the well. And, taking other camels with him, he went on to the girl's tribe. And when he was come, the girl said again, "I know not whether he be my bridegroom, but slay for him and serve to him the paunch and the tail, and give him to drink of the sour milk, and spread his bed upon the offal." But 'Imr-el-Káis refused, and called aloud to them that they should bring him of the liver and the hump, and of the fresh milk and the curds, and that they should build a tent for him on the clean ground. And she sent to him, asking the same questions she had asked of the slave. And 'Imr-el-Káis made answer, "My two lips are for the drinking of wine, my two sides are for the wearing of fine garments, and my two thighs for the riding of horses of noble blood." And she said, "This is my bridegroom. Slay ye the slave." And they slew him; and 'Imr-el-Káis went in to her.

Draught-playing, or perhaps more correctly backgammon. The name of the game in the Arabic is *El Nard*, which seems to have been played with dice.

The *Kitáb el Aghâni*. The "Book of Songs," a collection made by Imám 'Abulfáraj el 'Isfaháni, a learned Arabian of Ispahan, in the third century of the Héjra. His work is considered the principal authority on all matters connected with The Ignorance.

Tághleb and Bekr. These two tribes were equally descended from Wâïl; and 'Imr-el-Káis was connected with Tághleb through his mother. They are the same tribes that later came to blows and brought their complaints before 'Amr Ibn Hínd, occasioning the Odes of Amr Ibn Kolthúm and El Hârith.

Over and above the usual blood-price. The usual blood-price at the present day in Arabia is reckoned at from forty to fifty camels. For a great chief, however, the price of many lives may be required. In the case of Héjr's death, Héjr being king and ruler of the tribe which had revolted and slain him, the offer of a single life to be delivered over to his son was hardly a sufficient satisfaction, and it is not to be wondered at that 'Imr-el-Kâis refused. He spent a night, however, considering the proposal "in agitation," for his filial duty clearly demanded of him more than this, while his somewhat lukewarm friends were in favour of his accepting.

A well-known Idol. This was *Thul Khólsa*, the patron of safety, whom the pre-Islamic Arabs used to consult in their affairs of peace and war. The form of consultation was, as described in the text, by casting a sheaf of three arrows on the ground before the idol, and taking an omen from the figures made by them as they fell. 'Imr-el-Káis' anger with the idol shows the slight respect in which the supernatural was held by the pagan Arabs, and is very characteristic. The casting of arrows was also a common form of gambling.

El Móndir King of Híra . . . sent horsemen against him. There was an old family feud between the Kings of Kíndi and the Kings of Híra, the cause of which is thus given in the Kitáb el Aghani:

In the days when El Hárith Ibn Héjr was King of Kíndi, and El Móndir Ibn Ma-el-Samá was King of Híra, and the Késra Kabád el Feyrúz was on the throne of Persia, there appeared at the Persian Court a certain teacher of new doctrine, named Márdak; and this Márdak preached the duality of God (as a Spirit of good and a Spirit of evil), and also the community of women, and to the extent that no man should refuse his wife to another. And Kabád was converted to these doctrines, and he called upon El Móndir as his vassal to adopt them likewise, and also on El Hárith. And El Hárith consented to his wish, but El Móndir refused. And for this reason Kabád deposed El Móndir from his government, and appointed El Hárith to rule Híra in his stead. And it happened that one day Kabád was sitting with his wife, the mother of his son Anúshirwán, and Márdak made demand for the queen to satisfy his lust. And the Késra consented. But Anúshirwán was indignant at the insult offered to his mother, and besought of Márdak that he would not do this thing, even to the kissing of Márdak's foot. And Márdak yielded to him. But the bitterness remained in Anúshirwán's soul. And when Kabád died and Anúshirwán reigned in his stead, Anúshirwán took vengeance on Márdak and on his sect, the Zándakis, and he had them destroyed, and he restored El Móndir to his kingdom. And he sent Persian horsemen with El Móndir to drive out El Hárith from the government of Híra, and with them men of the Béni Tághleb and the Báhra and the Eyyád, and El Móndir pursued El Hárith even to the land of Koléyb, and the Béni Tághleb took from El Hárith his treasure and his riding camels and forty-eight of the men of his house. And El Móndir slew these forty-eight at Háfar el Amlák in the land of Mazína. And it is of this doing that Amr ibn Kolthúm sings:

"And they came back with plunder and captives and the sons of kings in chains."

The two hills of Táï. The Jébeleyn Táï, 'Aja and Sélma, now known as Jébel Shámmar, in the heart of Nejd. The two mountain ranges are of red granite separated by a plateau some thirty miles across, and 4,000 feet above the sea, the hills themselves being perhaps 2,000 feet higher. In ancient times this region was the home of the noble tribe of Táï, celebrated through the personal distinction of their hero Hátim Táï, the prince of hospitality. Hátim flourished a little later than the days of 'Imr-el-Káis. It is related of him, among other instances of his generosity, that one of the *Kayásira*, the Roman Emperors, having heard of Hátim's free-handedness, in order to make trial of it, sent his chamberlain to Nejd secretly to ask of him his mare, a mare known to be very precious to him. And the chamberlain alighted at Hátim's tent unannounced, and alone. And it happened that the flocks and the herds were away, and Hátim had no meat to set before his guest. And, seeing that he had no meat, he went out and slew his mare and kindled a fire and dressed the meat of her. And when his guest was satisfied, Hátim ask him of his errand. And he told him that he was Caesar's messenger, and made request for the mare. And Hátim was grieved, saying: "But if I had learned it before thou hadst dined!" And the chamberlain was astonished at what Hátim had done, and he returned and told the Emperor, and the Emperor said, "Verily we had heard much of him. But this is more than we had heard."

The tribe of Táï is no longer to be found in Nejd, their ancient seat being now occupied by the Shámmar. A section, however, of them still holds its own, as a clan of special nobility, in Mesopotamia, where it honourably preserves the tradition of Hátim, with something of his open-handedness, and a large custom of hospitality.

A certain valorous Jewish Chieftain. Before the preaching of Islam, though the mass of the Arabs had very little religion of any kind, and that little idolatrous, a considerable number of them professed Judaism, while others, especially in the north, were nominally Christian. Of the latter was the tribe of Ghassán, which later sided with the Roman Empire against the Mohammedan invaders of Syria. There seems to have been a general tolerance in the Peninsula for all religions. It is doubtful whether El Samúeli and others like him were Jews by race or only by religion. They were clearly accounted Arabs in general estimation, and were probably of Ishmaelitish descent. While Judaism has entirely disappeared from Central and Northern Arabia, it is still adhered to by a large community in Yémen. Christianity has been wholly extirpated throughout the Peninsula.

Dakhúli and Haúmali. The translators have taken the liberty, where the metre requires it, of printing proper names with the terminal vowels they receive in Arabic when placed in declension. Thus the mountains here spoken of would in the nominative be Dakhúl and Haúmal and only in the accusative Dakhúli and Haúmali. The metre, however, of the original is largely composed of proper names thus terminally declined, and there seems to be no positive reason in English for not also declining them.

Where the South and North winds crossweave the sand furrows. The *Nefúd*, or sand-dunes of Central Arabia cover immense tracts of country, in some places as much as 200 miles across, and to the depth of 200 and 300 feet. The naked crests of the ridges are being perpetually woven into new shapes by the wind, while the general features of the dunes vary little, overgrown as they are by a sparse but hardy vegetation. The Nefúds, except for their lack of water, are by no means the most arid portions of the desert, and supply not only good camel and sheep pasture, but also several kinds of grass good for horses. They are consequently a favourite home of the tribes, especially in the winter season, when these find shelter from the wind in the *felúj*, or hollows which are a feature of the deep sand formation, and fuel for their fires. In the winter the tribes need little water.

See the white-doe droppings. This couplet and the following, though only in the margin of Záuzani's version occur in the text of Tabrízi, and contain too much local colour to be lightly rejected; the phrase "fine grain of peppercorns" exactly represents the droppings of the gazelle which is here translated "doe" or, as in the English version of the Old Testament, "roe," though really the gazelle is no deer but an antelope.

Tears as of colocynth. Literally, "like one bruising the seeds of *hóndal*." The hóndal, or colocynth, is a wild melon which grows commonly in the desert. When green it has an attractive appearance, and is eaten greedily by the gazelle, but its fruit is of such extreme bitterness that it has always been a symbol of pain and grief to the Arabs, while its juice is so acrid as to affect to tears the eyes of the gatherer. Such at least is the popular belief.

Garánfoli. The wild stock or gillyflower, *garófalo* in Italian, an abundant herb in all the northern pastures, and esteemed as an excellent green meat, *éshub*, in Spring for the camels.

Howdah. The *hówdaj* or curtained camel-pannier in which Bedouin women sit travelling, a wide cradle, capable of holding two or more persons, and arched over with hoops on which carpets are spread as a protection from the sun. It is a picturesque structure often highly ornamented and always an object full of pleasant domestic associations to Bedouin eyes. *Khídra, ghabít* and *háudaj* are the terms used for it, rendered here alike by the Anglo-Indian form of the latter word "howdah."

Slave of grief. A rendering of his name, 'Imr-el-Káis (see note above).

Let him be, thy camel. This verse is of doubtful authenticity, being omitted from the versions alike of Tabrízi and Záuzani, and found only in the collection called *Jámhurat el 'Arab.* It is interesting from the phrase "grudge not my croup-riding," which illustrates the common Bedouin practice of climbing on the camel's croup, in the case of a second rider, which doubtless was 'Imr-el-Káis' way when wishing to converse with those in the hówdaj.

Clove-apples. Safárjali, a quince with a clove-like flavour.

The Pleiades. El thoráyya, the lights, perhaps in allusion to the seven-branched candlestick. 'Imr-el-Kais' simile will remind readers of Tennyson's couplet:

> "Many a night I saw the Pleiads, rising through the mellow shade,
> Glitter like a swarm of fire-flies tangled in a silver braid."

Thus are pearls yet virgin. Some of the commentators read this passage as a comparison not to pearls but to an ostrich-egg, for the word *mukanáti* in the text may mean either. The context, however, with the allusion to water, makes it pretty certain that pearls are intended. Pearls were, of course, very familiar to the Arabs who had a close connection through Bahréyn with the Persian Gulf, where the best pearl-fisheries of ancient times were found. Another reading is *bardíyu,* the water-lily. But *mukanáti* signifies anything of a white colour tinged with yellow.

White as an ariel's. The *rîm* or *áriel* antelope, larger than the common *dorcas* antelope, both being gazelles. The ariel is rare now in Arabia and has assumed there a semi-fabulous character.

Fluted as water-worms. These are daring similes, all having a local significance. The tooth-sticks, *masawîk,* are made of the *Isbal* tree.

Dragged with his hind feet halting. This metaphor is very characteristic of the camel's motion. When tired or unwilling, he seems to be leaving his hind-legs behind him while his fore-hand goes on.

Water-skins of some folks. This couplet stands rather out of connection with those next it, and very likely has been shifted from its right position. Its reference is to the help given to the women of the tribe when bringing skins of water from the wells, and which is often a form of courtship used by young Bedouins. The verse occurs in Záuzani but not in all versions.

Red-bay he. Kométy is the Arabic word. It is usually held to have been used of a very dark bay, what the French call "bai brun." But Sheykh Mohammed Abdu insists that the colour is really a very dark chestnut "alezan brulé." The word *koméyt* is no longer used in Arabia in connection with either colour and must be considered obsolete in its application to horses.

As spent fishes swim. The term "swimming" is commonly applied in Arabian poetry to the gallopping of horses.

A hermit, pouring oil-sésame. The hermit's lamp is a constant simile with the pre-Islamic poets, and doubtless has reference to the early Christian anchorites who in the fifth and sixth centuries peopled the caves and tombs of certain vallies of the desert. They lived on the alms of the faithful, and hung out their lamps at night to attract charitable strangers. Though protected by a special command of the Prophet, they became involved in the religious persecutions of the age that followed, and for more security congregated within walled buildings, the first Christian monasteries. Such still exist in their primitive condition at Mount Sinai, St. Anthony's and elsewhere, some of them in extremely remote places. The anchorites have ceased to live on alms and are usually possessed of farms in the cultivated districts which supply their necessities.

The Kanábboli. The Kanáhbol tree, it is uncertain of what kind.

The Ibexes. The ibex, *bédden*, the wild goat of Scripture, is found in all the rocky districts of Arabia, at an altitude of from two thousand to six thousand feet above the sea, though not on the plains. In the higher mountains it may be said to be still plentiful, keeping as near the crests of the hills as the necessity of its pasturing allows. Its lairs are almost always on high ground where it keeps vigilant watch; but in severe weather, such as that described in the text, it is driven down into the vallies. The Bedouins hunt it with their greyhounds who drive it to bay, usually on the face of a precipice, where it is easily secured. Unlike the wild-sheep, *kebsh móyeh*, which, it is said, never drinks, the ibex needs water constantly in summer.

Thablra and Mujéymir. Mountains in Northern Nejd, not far from Téyma, where Imr el Káis' Jewish protector had his castle.

NOTES ON TÁRAFA.

Tárafa. The *Jámhuret Ashâar el 'Arab* of Mufáddal, one of the earliest commentators, gives his proper name as 'Amr Ibn Abd, stating that Tárafa was a pseudonym. But this is not generally accepted, nor is the meaning of *Tárafa*, if it be a nickname, clear.

Dhébya. A branch of the great tribe of Békr, descended from the patriarch Robía.

Bahréyn. An island and seaport on the coast of the Persian Gulf, renowned for its pearl fisheries. Bahréyn is the traditional first home of the Phoenicians, from which, according to Herodotus, they migrated to the Mediterranean, maintaining, however, for many centuries a trade connection with the Gulf. To the Phoenicians, who were skilled in mechanical arts, the caravan traders crossing Arabia owe in all probability their wells, some of them being as deep as 300 feet. The Phoenicians also left inscriptions on the sandstone rocks, to which allusion is sometimes made in the ancient Arabic poetry. Bahréyn has for the most part been a dependency of the Persian monarchy, and in Tárafa's time was governed by a lieutenant of the kings of Híra, themselves dependent on the Késra. In our own day the family of Ibn Khalífa, its chief ruler, has been noted for its horses, derived principally from the Ajmán tribes of the mainland. Ottoman rule was established there in 1875.

A Christian of the Ebádi. The poet Mutalémmis, Tárafa's mother's brother, is said to have been a Christian Arab, and his name, Abd-el-Messíh, Slave of the Messiah, is given in evidence. The Ebádi would seem to have been townsmen of Híra and so acquainted with writing.

Kháula. According to the commentator Hishám ibn el Kélbi, this lady was of his own tribe of Kelb, but nothing more is known of her than that she was the beloved of Tárafa.

Dyed dark as the hands of her. Indigo markings in patterns on hands and face are usual with Bedouin women. They are supposed to preserve the skin from sun-burning. Thus, too, the "dark-lipped one" of the text.

Ships tall-rigged from Adáuli. Adáuli, a port of Bahréyn on the mainland. Ibn Yámin is said to have been a noted shipbuilder there. This passage has suggested the idea that Tárafa composed his Ode at Bahréyn. The simile is a fine one, and exactly represents the converging of the lines of camels at the *ráhla*, when, leaving their separate camping grounds, the tribeswomen come together in their howdahs for the morning's march.

Sand heaped by the sand-seers. The *mufáïl*, or sand-diviners, took their omens from pebbles heaped over with sand, which they then parted into two with their hands, and, according as the pebbles were found in one or the other heaps, so they decided small matters of divination, such as the fortunate direction of the march, the chances of misadventure, and the presence of an enemy. The practice is still followed.

A striped cloak. This is a simile which those who have travelled much along the desert caravan-roads will at once recognize as a true one. These roads show sometimes as many as a hundred parallel camel paths, making a very distinct striped pattern, like the búrjud or striped cloak worn by the Arabs, traversing the plains.

The ash-plumed proud lord of her. Alluding apparently to the male ostrich, though "ash-plumed," *árbadi*, seems hardly appropriate to the male, whose colouring is black, white, and red.

Scared by the thick-furred red-thief. A wild beast of some sort, probably a fox. Commentators, however, generally explain it to mean the male camel. The brandishing of the tail is a sign of anger or impatience in a camel, and is likened in the text to "*a falcon, the wings of him bating her flanks impatient.*" This is absurdly interpreted in most of the commentaries as a "white eagle." But it is quite clear that it refers to the habit of carrying a falcon for hawking purposes behind the camel saddle. The lashing of the tail reminds the poet of the "bating" or beating of the wings of the hawk held there by the jesses. Captain Johnson renders this passage in his translation, "as if the two wings of a white vulture enclosed the sides of it (*i.e.*, her tail) pierced into the bone of the tail by means of an awl."

Red chestnut. The finest running camels of Northern Arabia, those bred by the Sherarát, are often of this colour, *sobábiyat.* The best Ománi camels of the south are white.

High as in ships of Díjleh The Arabic form of the river Tigris is "Díjleh," apparently a corruption, on one side or other, of the same word.

Roman builded. The ancient Arabs had no art of building in stone. Their castles were always the work of Roman, *i.e.*, Greek masons, brought from the north, *el Rum.*

Ears fearful of the night sounds. The ears of a camel always betray her fears. When anxious they stand out at right angles with her head.

A test stone. Mirdát was, according to the commentators, a stone used for breaking other stones upon. But the passage is an obscure one.

Nose pierced for nose-ring. The riding-camel, besides her halter, has a light string attached to a loop passed through the cartilage of the nostril. When held in, this draws back her head to the knee-crutch of the rider, whereas, going at speed, her head is carried low, on a level with her knees.

A branch of Khirwa. The palma Christi, set often, on account of its extremely rapid growth, by the side of temporary watering pits. In a couple of months it is possible to sit under its shade, as Jonah sat under his gourd.

We cast the arrows gaily. This too is an obscure passage, and one omitted in some versions. It seems to refer to a game of chance in which the arrows were thrown on the ground, not by the players, but by a third person, called the *mújmid.* Others, however, say that the *mújmid* was the stakeholder. The arrows were of a yellow wood, their points hardened in the fire.

Once on a time I bound me. The order in which the concluding verses are given varies in different versions, and some of them do not occur in all. The arrangement, however, followed here seems most consonant with the sense of the poem.

Only shall One bring tidings. The meaning of this is much disputed, but it pretty clearly refers to Death. Some Moslem commentators have affected to see in it a prophecy of Mohammed's coming.

NOTES ON ZOHÉYR.

I will strike thee beneath the ear-rings. The threat, "I will cut off thy head," is one in common use among the Arabs in emphasizing an order. It is not intended seriously.

And the horse stumbled and fell. The power of the eye was one of the few superstitions of the Pagan Arabs, just as it is still among thc modern Bedouins. There are few who do not believe that certain persons are able by their envious eyes to strike down either horse or camel.

Slant-wise up El Subáan they mounted. This and the following couplets are somewhat freely translated in the text. The literal rendering should be, according to Captain Johnson: "And they inclined towards the valley of Soobán, ascending the centre of it, and in their faces were the fascinating looks of a soft-bodied person brought up in easy circumstances."

House revered of Koréysh and Júrhum. The Káaba at Mecca is traditionally held to have been built by the tribal ancestor of the Koréysh who had taken to wife a daughter of Júrhum, thus uniting the two great stems descended from Ismaíl and Kahtán, the Ishmaël and Joktan of the Hebrew scriptures.

Ye Lords of Mórra. El Hárith and Hárim, the chieftains who made the peace. They, in common with the rest of the Yémenite clans, were descended from Maád.

Your ear-marked ones. This refers to the tribal markings, *wusúm*, set upon all camels born within the tribe, each tribe having its own manner of slitting the ears. The poet distinguishes these home-bred camels as of more value than the camels captured in war.

For ye may not hide from God your dealings. In both Zohéyr's and Lebíd's Odes certain pious expressions occur which suggest that the couplets containing them may have been added after their conversion to Islam. There was no piety in Pagan Arabia.

Twins hath she borne to you. The rendering "twins" here is not quite correct, the original having "two boys," *ghilmán*. The camel very seldom produces twins, and almost as seldom a foal two years running. The phrase which immediately follows, "she is quickly weaned of them," would seem to imply that the camel has produced a second foal before she has weaned the first.

Aád's. 'Ahmar of Aád, who slew the camel of the Prophet Sáleh, as related in the Koran. The commentators consider that "Ahmar of Thamúd" should be substituted as more consonant with the sacred text.

No such plenty Irák hath garnered. Irák, which is the province watered by the Lower Euphrates and Tigris, had Ctesiphon at that time for capital. It was cultivated by a vast system of canal irrigation, now fallen to decay, which made it the richest corn-producing district, after Egypt, of the ancient world. Its prosperity was well maintained under the Arabian Caliphate, which made of it the chief seat of the Moslem Government. But in the thirteenth century it was overwhelmed by the Tartar invasion under Hologú, who destroyed nearly the entire agricultural population. The canals then fell into ruin and have never since been repaired.

Om-Káshami. The vulture-mother, a common symbol of war, and the calamities of war.

Pure of blood, Nahík's. It was on account of the slaying of Ibn Nahík that the quarrel between Abs and Dobián began. Muthéllem, Náufal, Wáhab and Mukházzem were all chieftains of Abs slain in the war.

That he who shall refuse the lance-butts. The Bedouin rider carries his lance, a hollow bamboo cane fourteen to sixteen feet long, over his shoulder in time of peace, the point of it behind him and the butt, which is also shod with iron, but bluntly, in front. When fighting he reverses it, using it not under-handed as our European lancers do, but over-handed, brandished and shaken above his head. Thus the Norman knights are represented in the Bayeux tapestry. It is in this way a much more formidable weapon in the hand of a fine rider, as it can be used on the near as easily as on the off side of the horse, and can also on occasion be hurled as a javelin. The sword is only used by the Bedouins when dismounted. Fire-arms thirty years ago were almost unknown among the great horse-owning tribes of Nejd, but are now more common, to the growing detriment of their horse-breeding. In the hill country of Hejáz and Yémen match-locks have long been in use, but in these districts the tribes are mainly camel-riders or go on foot.

There was a certain great lord of Dóbián. This beautiful story is adapted from Sir Charles Lyall's translation.

Perfumes of Minshami. Mínsham is said to have been a lady who sold perfumes at Mecca, and at whose house certain young men made an oath, plunging their hands in a perfumed bowl, binding them to stand together in a quarrel; carrying out which engagement all were killed.

NOTES ON LEBÍD.

Yea, all that is is vain. These verses are given on the authority of Mr. Clouston, who quotes them, in another form, from Sir Charles Lyall. Their tone, however is so little that of the true pagan poet that they can hardly be authentic. They are repudiated by modern Mohammedan criticism.

This is that táriba. It has been impossible to identify the shrub here alluded to among the many desert plants to which the description might apply.

A shedád or camel-saddle. The Bedouins of Arabia ride on a saddle with two crutches, sitting side-ways. The *shedád* consists of a frame-work of wood with two separate trees, each surmounted by a knobbed crutch, the one in front of, the other behind the hump, and connected together by side-pieces of wood bound with thongs loosely so as to allow of a certain play, corresponding with the motion of the camel's back, the whole covered with a leathern pad, and that again with a pair of highly ornamented camel-bags with tassels and fringes. It forms a comfortable riding-seat, and figures also, when not required for riding, as a seat or rest on which to lean in the tent. The passage does not necessarily imply that Lebíd sat all night on his camel—rather on the camel-saddle placed on the ground, where he was keeping watch.

Years how long, the war-months, months too of peace-pleasures. The Arabian year was divided, before the time of Mohammed, into eight fighting months and four months of peace, the *halál* and the *harám*. Hence the "forbidden" month, *Mohárrem*, retained in the Islamic Calendar.

Fresh-spilled from the Zodiac. The houses of the sun, *menázil*, literally the sun's "camping grounds," an expression commonly used of the Zodiac.

As one paints a maid's cheek. In allusion to the patterns tattooed in indigo on a girl's face. This is a universal practice.

Thorn-bush fencing. When a Bedouin tent is pitched, bushes are collected and used to fill up the gap between the tent-wall and the ground; and, where the camp is intended to be at all permanent, a *zariba* is constructed of the same material in which to fold the lambs and kids during the day-time when their dams are away grazing. In the text a particular thorn-bush, the *themám*, is mentioned.

Every howdah curtained. Although Bedouin girls and old women go freely without veil or other show of concealment beyond that of being restricted when at home to their own half of the tent, divided from the men's half by a low curtain, a certain coquetry is displayed in regard to the young married women, with whom it has always been considered a mark of distinction that they should be kept somewhat out of sight and hidden at least from the eyes of strangers when travelling. Hence the insistance in all the poems on the curtaining of the howdahs and the closeness of the concealment, when those specially loved are remembered.

Fled as the mirage flees. The word in the text, *saráb*, is that commonly used for the false appearance of water seen in the desert, and which Europeans call "mirage." The word "mirage" may possibly have been derived by travellers from the Arabic *meráj*, meadows, which are sometimes a form of the appearance, but the word as applied to the appearance itself is not an Arabic one.

'Ithel and rock-mazes. The *'Ithel* tree belongs to the same family as the tamarisk, *tárfa*, but is a larger and more valuable tree, its timber being in much request in the Nejd towns. It grows there to a height of about thirty feet, with a girth of as much as eight or ten feet. It is not very different from the *ábel* of Egypt, a graceful tree with a light feathery foliage.

Eastward move they marching . . . camped in Tái. This passage is interesting geographically as indicating the locality of the scene described in the poem. The two hills of Tái, are the modern ranges of Jébel Shámmar, while Fáïda is a still existing oasis south of Jébel Sélma. It is not difficult, therefore, to place the valley of Lebíd's parting somewhere in Northern Nejd between Háïl and Téyma. All the names might perhaps with pains be made out by the modern traveller, or rather the traveller of the future, for as yet the valleys of Nejd have been hardly if ever visited by strangers. The translators traversed this part of Nejd in the year 1879.

Her hide shoe-straps. On long journeys over rocky ground, especially in the heat of summer, the Bedouins shoe their running camels with sandals, *khidám*, attached with thongs to the fetlocks. These are soon worn through and need constant renewing.

A fair wild-ass. *Múlmi* in the text, signifying a she-ass in foal, the usual word for the she-ass being *atán*. In the same way the ass-stallion is here called *ábkab*, meaning the "white-flanked one," the ordinary name for the male wild-ass being *a-ir*. The wild ass of Asia, though not believed to be the progenitor of our tame stock, is nevertheless distinctly of the ass tribe. It is found now on the central plains of Persia, in upper Mesopotamia, and in Nejd, but is there confined to certain hill ranges, notably to Jébel Towéyk, where it maintains a precarious existence. The Nejd plateaux contain at least four grasses, besides a number of other plants, fit for the pasturage alike of asses and horses; and the wild ass is a frugal feeder. But in the summer time he needs water, and it is at that season that the hunters take him in their ambushes, *merákeb*. These are stone circles, built in certain places where wild animals are in the habit of passing, either as hiding places for the hunter, or, where gazelles are concerned, as pits into which they may be jostled by their companions in the herd when alarmed. The gazelles at certain seasons of the year migrate in immense flocks, and then is the hunter's opportunity.

Six months of Jumáda. The six months of Winter and Spring, an old reckoning, during which the wild animals of the desert do not need water. With the approach of summer, however, they are driven by their thirst to the springs in the hills and the deep clefts found in all the lime-stone districts, at the bottom of which rain-water will remain sweet and good for a year or two years, or even in some for three and four years unreplenished. The springs, on the contrary, such as the spring described in the text, "all its banks a cane-brake," are seldom very drinkable. The water in them is clear but brackish, so much so that in Arabia clearness in water is almost always a sign of its bad quality. Such as it is, however, it is drunk by the wild beasts as well as by the camels, to whom salt is a necessity of their well-being. Certain animals are said never to drink, the hare, the fénnek-fox, no larger than a rabbit, the gazelle and the wild-sheep, perhaps also the oryx antelope.

With heels wounded. In the text "wounded by the *sáfa*," a thorny plant of desert growth.

Or a wild-cow wolf-raided. The oryx antelope, which from its cow-like tail, shoulder hump, white colour and other features, is considered a cow by the Arabs. The horns of the oryx are three feet long, perfectly straight and sharp-pointed, and good weapons of defence. The animal is still fairly abundant in all the great sand deserts, Nefúds, of Central Arabia, and in company with gazelles, may be seen in captivity in the gardens of great personages at Háïl and elsewhere. These have doubtless been captured young. The desert wolf, which ranges from the Euphrates to the Nile, is an animal of wide-roving habits, identical, or nearly so, with the wolf of Europe. It is a large and powerful beast, and will attack fearlessly the sheep folded in the tents at night, or even by day. But it never goes in packs as the wolf does in Upper Asia, and so is seldom dangerous to man. It must not be confounded with the jackal, which is not a true desert dweller, and which is, we believe, never found in Arabia proper, though plentifully in the borderlands of Syria, Mesopotamia and the Nile Valley.

Freed from the string of it. The commentators explain this rather obscure passage as alluding to the restlessness of the wild cow, which is likened to a pearl loosed from its string and rolling this way and that. The explanation seems, however, far-fetched. It is more probable that it means simply a single pearl parted from the other pearls of a necklace, and so perhaps more distinctly seen in the darkness.

Twin spears of Sámbar. Sámhar is said to have been a noted spear-maker at Bahréyn, the seaport where bamboos for the purpose were imported into Arabia. At the present day bamboos are procured mostly from Bássorah.

Kasábi and Sukhám. Proper hound-names, feminine and masculine. The greyhounds are spoken of as "the lop-eared," *ghodfán*, to distinguish them from the prick-eared sheep-dogs.

Ay, and love's sunderer. The young Arabs of the Ignorance took a pride in divorcing readily. There are many tales told of divorces on very slight grounds.

Drank at the flag-hoisting, drank till the wine grew dear. The wine formerly drunk in Arabia came mostly from Syria and was conveyed to Nejd in goat-skins or jars lined with resin, just as wine barrels are still resined in Greece. The travelling retailers were principally Christians, who hoisted a flag at their tent door to signify that liquor was for sale. This brought the revellers round them, and the skins were put up to auction and emptied on the spot.

Fingering the lute-strings. In the text a "corded instrument" only is named, but doubtless this was the lute, *el úd* in Arabic, whence its European name.

On what dawns sharp-winded. This is another obscure passage, meaning in all probability that the poet kept his friends warm in winter by feasting them.

Dun-red the slopes of them. The sand of the great Nefúds is of a strong red colour, its texture coarser than that of the white sands.

I who their shares portioned, drawing the lots for them. When a camel was slain for guests, the entertainer divided the meat into a number of portions which were distributed by lot.

Nágas at a tomb tied. In pagan times, when a chief died, his riding-camel was knee-haltered and left to die at his tomb.

NOTES ON ÁNTARA.

The slur of illegitimacy. Among the noble tribes of Nejd, though concubinage sometimes occurs with a slave woman, the offspring is not accorded the rights of a free-born Arab, nor can a man so born obtain an Arab girl to wife. Indeed, the issue of all marriages outside the tribe is considered illegitimate, and when a tribesman takes a stranger to wife he usually makes his abode with her people, having become an outcast from his own. 'Antara's aspiration, therefore, to the hand of his cousin was an abnormal incident, and was equivalent to a claim of legitimacy. Among the Bedouins, marriages between cousins are the rule, not the exception, and the custom is that a marriageable girl must obtain the consent of all her first cousins before she can contract with one of another family. So prevalent, indeed, is the marriage of first cousins, that it is common for a husband, even if his wife is unrelated to him in blood, to address her as *bint ámmi*, "daughter of my uncle." These close intermarriages, where there is perfect health on both sides, seem to be in no way hurtful. They have, at any rate, been practised among the most vigorous tribes from time immemorial. 'Antara's quarrel with his family was that he conceived himself to have a right to Abla as a birth-right.

Light-handed smithy-strokes. In the text "short-handed." But this is probably a corrupt version. The explanations given by the commentators have no reasonable meaning; and the rendering "light-handed" must be preferred. Captain Johnson's translation of this and the preceding couplet is as follows:

> "The fly alone enjoyed it, and so did not cease humming as is the act of the singing drunkard;
> Humming, while he rubs one fore-leg against the other, as the striking on the flint of one, bent on the flint, and cut off as to his palm."

A swift Shadanleb. Doubtless the name in the feminine of a breed of running camels, by the commentators said to be of Yémen. Thus at the present day the breeds *Sherarleb*, *Omanleh*, *Azraghleh*. The camel is spoken of as "under ban for the drinker," meaning that her foal had been weaned from her.

The ear-less one. In the text the camel is compared to the *musállam*, that is to say the male ostrich, which the Arabs believe to be deaf. The ostrich, again, by a poverty of imagination not unfrequent in their similes, is compared in its turn to the camel, or rather a troop of young ostriches, led by a male ostrich in his black and white plumage, to a herd of she camels in charge of a slave, *ájemi*, literally, a stranger, who is called a "stammerer" because of his broken Arabic. At least such is the best meaning the commentators can read into the passage.

Scared by the hunting one. Here again is a most obscure simile, made more obscure by the explanations given of it. It seems, however, to the present translators that the passage refers to the use of the hunting leopard, *fábad*, to which there is a distinct reference in the Kitáb el Agháni as a custom of the ancient Arabs, the leopard being carried on the croup of the camel behind its keeper. Thus the meaning of the passage would be that the camel shrank from the enemy's pools as from a leopard placed on her back. It is difficult to understand the "led-cat" in any other sense. The description of the sweat oozing like pitch from her ear-roots is very characteristic.

Ask of the horsemen of Málek. Málek was the father of Abla, against whose kinsmen 'Antara had found himself at feud and had indeed killed not a few of them. It is to these that he appeals as witnesses to Abla of his valour.

Heavy his mail coat. The coat of mail was the only armour known to the Arabs, and it was they who, through Spain, introduced it into Europe. It is still occasionally used by them in their wars, but its weight is too great a disadvantage to them in their rapid manner of fighting for it ever to have become part of their common desert equipment. It was only the princes and great chieftains who were sufficiently well-mounted to carry it habitually.

Quick-handed he with the arrows cast in the winter time. The allusion here is most certainly to gambling.

The dark sons of Demdem. These are Huséyn Ibn Démdem and his kinsmen whose breach of the truce has been recorded in connection with Zohéyr's Ode.

NOTES ON AMR IBU KOLTHÚM.

Her father ordered her at her birth to be destroyed. It was an occasional practice among the Pagan Arabs to destroy female infants at their birth. This was doubtless on account of the chronic hunger in which the Bedouins lived and the great mortality among the males in their wars.

A poisonous wind, simúm. Though burning winds are prevalent at certain seasons of the year everywhere in the desert, it has been scientifically doubted whether poisonous winds ever really occur. Palgrave in the account of his journey to Nejd in 1863 gives an account of such a wind, in very graphic terms, as having overtaken his party between Maán and Jôf, but he stands alone among modern travellers as a believer in winds of an actually poisonous quality, apart from the sense of suffocation they no doubt produce. The translators have never themselves undergone any such experience or met with any Bedouin who has claimed such experience, though the existence of the *simúm* is generally believed in the desert, as it certainly was in ancient times by all travellers.

His hand became cut by the bow-string. It is not easy to ascertain at what date the bow ceased to be used in Bedouin warfare, nor the reason of its having ceased. It is not that the bow had been replaced by fire-arms, for among the great fighting tribes firearms are still practically unknown, or were so a generation back. Yet the use of the bow has not only long ceased, but the memory of it is entirely forgotten. Even the wandering hunting tribes, the Sleb, who must certainly have used it formerly, know nothing of it at the present day.

Andarina. This is an inflection of *Andarín*, the name of a district in Syria formerly noted for its wine, as also was Baalbék, *Baálabekki* in the text. The wine must have been white wine, for it is said to foam like *huss*, saffron. It was drunk hot by the ancient Arabs, and always mixed with water, as was also, and is still, the custom of the Greeks, whose modern name for wine is *krási*, a "mixture."

NOTES ON AMR IBU KOLTHÚM

Om Sákbin. The colt's mother, meaning the she-camel.

Lances black of the Khótti. The commentators say that this refers to a certain Khótti, or man of Khot, who was a well-known spear-maker.

Loads let loose on a road. This is a simile which everyone who has travelled with a camel caravan will recognize as a good one. The bales of merchandise are balanced on either side of the *badájeb* or pack-saddle, and held together with a cord. On this being loosened, the bales roll over on the ground to right and left.

As Madd well knoweth. Maád was the tribal patriarch of all the Yémenite Arabs. The phrase therefore means "as is known to all the tribes."

When surprise is our lot, and the tent-roofs tumble. It is a matter of pride with the warlike Arabs to be able in a very few minutes to move camp. On the sudden alarm of an enemy every tent in an encampment will be seen instantly to fall, so that all shall be ready for the march. To be attacked with the tents standing would be to invite confusion and defeat.

Ours the captain of Júshm. The word in the text is *rás*, "head," or war-leader, otherwise *akíd*, whence our European word "guide." This leader is not necessarily the head Sheykh of the tribe, though usually a member of the supreme family. Júshm ibn Békr, 'Alkama, Mohálhil, Zohéyr and the rest stand recorded in the tribal pedigree. It is a peculiarity of the Arabs that all, even the poorest, know their ancestry.

Who dares link our she-camel with his. This is an allusion to the habit in caravans of tying the camels head to tail. It is not practised in the tribal marches of the Bedouins which are made, each camel singly, in irregular line, but only on beaten tracks by the townsmen.

The strong-hold of Thú-urát. In Jebel 'Aja and elsewhere in Nejd there are certain enclosed valleys entered by narrow rock-passages which are used by the tribes as places of refuge. Within them are often palms and water, but little pasture. El Agdeh near Háïl, Ibn Rashíd's stronghold, is of this kind and was visited in 1879 by the translators.

The bend of our backs, where the armour pressed us, scored like waves. This is one of the passages whose meaning has been most disputed. It seems, however, to the translators as clearly referring to the wavy lines of the mail-links left on the backs of the wearers.

Lo the mares we bestride . . . are not these the inheritance of our fathers? This passage is of great interest as showing the tradition already existing in Arabia in pagan times of the great antiquity there of the horse, and may be cited in answer to those moderns who hold the horse to have been introduced into Arabia at a comparatively late date. Piétrement, though not the originator of the new heresy, is its principal exponent. According to him the Bedouins of Nejd obtained their first horses from the kings of Híra and Ghassán. But it is surely incredible that, had such been the case, 'Amr ibn Kolthúm, while pleading before a king of Híra, should have indulged in a boast such as stands in the text. Nothing is clearer from the Poetry of the Ignorance than that the Arab idea about their horses, as an indigenous possession, was precisely in their day what it now is in ours. The mention, too, which is so frequent, of mares being used in their wars, may be contrasted with a common assertion that in ancient Arabia horses only were used. What is probable is that in the days when armour was more commonly used than now, the armoured chiefs rode stallions in battle as being more powerful weight-carriers. On their long expeditions, however, it is clear that mares were always preferred for the same reasons that they are now.

The shredding of limbs, like a plaything shredded. The word here given as "plaything," in the text *kulát*, is somewhat obscure. It has generally been interpreted as a kind of hockey, possibly polo; according to Captain Johnson, tip-cat. None of these games, however, correspond exactly to the sense of the text, which the translators imagine to have been a pumpkin slashed in sword-play. The only games now played by Bedouin children are with a rude ball either struck with a stick or with the foot.

Lo, the seas we will sack with our war-galleys. This seems to be a prophecy of future expansion rather than a statement of anything that had been already done by the tribe. The piracy on the sea-coasts of Arabia is the work, not of the great pastoral tribes, but rather of the villagers of the littoral. Nevertheless the principle of the Arab pirate-raids by sea is precisely the same as that of their *ghazús* by land, a principle which supposes each tribe to be a nation at war with all other nations unless protected by treaty. The international law of Europe has a very similar basis.

NOTES ON EL HARÍTH.

Our kind kin the Arákim. 'Amr ibn Kolthúm's tribal section was called *El Arákim*, the Speckled Snakes. Most of the older tribal names of Arabia are derived from animals or other natural objects, as were those of the Red Indians of America. Thus we have still existing the *'Anazeh* and *Maázeh*, goats; the *Sherarát*, butterflies; the *Sebáa*, lions; and the *Beni Mutéyr*, children of the rain. Professor Robertson Smith believed these to have been originally the totems of the tribes.

All that have run with us the wild ass. Here *aïr* is the word used. The meaning is "all that have hunted in our company."

O thou King Iramíyan. Irám was one of Ibn Hind's ancestors.

Closing lids on our wrong though the mote lie under. A fine trope. As though it were said, "We shut our eyes on our wrong, though the wrong still wounds us."

Blackness burnt in the sun. Alluding to the *Harra*, a black volcanic region extending from Damascus in the north, intermittently in a narrow strip, as far as Medina in the south. Its labyrinth of black boulders has at all times served as a place of refuge both for the oppressed and for evil-doers. It is a region of intense heat in the summer.

Lo, how stiff was our stand for him, El Móndir. This is an allusion to a war made by the Béni-Bekr, in alliance with El Móndir, King of Híra, Ibn Hind's father, against El Hárith, King of Ghassán. The quarrel was an old one, and in the course of it El Hárith, having lost a battle, sent a certain Shámmar of the Hanífa tribe to treat of peace, but with a secret instruction to seize any opportunity of unguardedness to take blood-vengeance. This man of Hanífa accordingly went to El Móndir's camp, and while there found an occasion and slew him, capturing also El Móndir's son, Imr-el-Kais, who must not be confused with Imr-el-Kais the poet. Upon this the Béni-Bekr joined Ibn Hind against Ghassán, and released Imr-el-Káis from their hands, killing one of their kings, whose daughter, Maisúna, they at the same time made captive and brought to Ibn Hind. She is the Maisúna referred to in the poem, and for whom Ibn Hind built the tent, and who "so loved Ausá-u," her early home in Ghassán.

First when came from Shakík at him the war-lords. This refers to the "Day of Shakík," when Káis Ibn Mádi Kéreb, with a large force from Yémen, raided the camels of Ibn Hind, but was driven back with loss by the Béni-Bekr. Shakík is a solitary watering-place, also visited by the translators, with three wells in the middle of the great sand desert between Jôf and Háïl. The wells are 300 feet deep. Káis is spoken of in the poem as the "Karathíyan," from the *kárath* tree found in Yémen, a sort of oak used for tanning.

Then trembled deep our spears in their well, like a long-roped bucket. The comparison of spears to well-ropes is one constantly occurring in Arabian poetry, generally on account of their length and slenderness. In the present instance, however, allusion also is made to the trembling of a long rope with a weight attached to it, and which reminds the poet of the trembling of the spears when shaken above their heads by the horsemen charging.

Next with Hójra it was. This records an expedition made by one of the kings of Kíndi against Híra, when the Béni-Bekr had again given Híra their assistance. The Iráni in the text were a body of Persian horsemen who marched with Hojra.

When Jaun of Aál Béni 'Aus sought us. This Jaun was another of the kings of Kíndi defeated by the Béni-Bekr in alliance with Híra. Jaun's two sons were made prisoners on the occasion.

Lastly brought we the nine of tho blood royal. The tale to which this refers is told in the text of the biography. It relates to the capture of the nine sons of Hejr 'Akil el Marár, brothers of the poet Imr-el-Kais, who were brought by the Béni-Bekr to El Móndir, when the king had them put to death outside the city of Híra.

'Amr a son was of ours, Ibn Om Eyyási. This 'Amr was 'Amr Ibn Hind's grandfather, his mother being Eyyás of the Béni-Bekr.

The Oath of Thil-Majázi. Thil-Majázi was the place in the Hejáz near Mecca where the Bekr and Taghleb agreed to the peace when Ibn Hind intervened between them, as is told in the biography.

That which stands on the skin. The parchment of the treaty. This passage shows that the treaty was put in writing, an unusual circumstance in Bedouin practice. But it must be remembered that the King of Híra was party to it, and that Híra lay on the confines of the civilised world. It cannot be taken as a proof that the Bedouin tribes themselves knew anything of letters more than they do now.

Take for vow of a sheep a gazelle in payment. The vow of killing a sheep is often made by the Bedouins in moments of danger. It would be held a base act not to fulfil the vow, or to elude it by killing something of lower value when the danger was over.

Eighty went of Temím. The stories to which the last verses of the poem refer are thrown in the teeth of the Béni Tághleb as instances of their misfortunes in war and their failures to obtain blood vengeance.

The Day of Hayáreyn. A great final battle in which Ibn Hind, with the assistance of Béni-Bekr was completely victorious.

www.ingramcontent.com/pod-product-compliance
Ingram Content Group UK Ltd.
Pitfield, Milton Keynes, MK11 3LW, UK
UKHW061539190726
13845UKWH00031B/1108

9 789366 081540